GOOD FRIENDS, JUST

GOOD FRIENDS, JUST

Anne Leaton

CHATTO & WINDUS

THE HOGARTH PRESS

LONDON

Published in 1983 by Chatto & Windus · The Hogarth Press
40 William IV Street, London WC2N 4DF

British Library Cataloguing in Publication Data

Leaton, Anne
Good friends, just.
I. Title
823'.914[F]   PR9051.E/

ISBN 0-7011-2710-4
ISBN 0-7011-2711-2 Pbk

Typeset by Inforum Ltd, Portsmouth
Printed in Great Britain by
Richard Clay, The Chaucer Press,
Bungay, Suffolk

TO FRIDA

GUNZEL PACED BACK AND FORTH FROM THE BENCH where Georgina sat to the weighing-in counter where no one was weighing anything in any more, all that being finished for the time being. She smoothed down her tweed coat and fidgeted with her handbag. When she got to the bench end of her route, where Georgina sat, she stopped and put one thin hand to her forehead. 'This country,' she said. 'It's going to kill me someday.'

Georgina's closed face opened a little. She smiled. She lifted her hands up and caressed the sides of her hair and ran one hand back over the knot of hair at the base of her skull. She was placid.

Maddy stood over by the door looking at a Türk Hava Yolari poster from which a pilot who looked like a Bauhaus lamp gazed over the edge into eternity.

Melek sat, smothered in a beige cape she had knitted herself, on the end of the same bench where Georgina sat. She was eating pistachios and thinking about something else entirely. She had her legs crossed at the ankles and tucked away inconspicuously under the bench. She knew that when the flight was finally called Gunzel would collect her from her reverie and deposit her where she should be. Melek had at all times a great faith.

'Waiting drives me crazy. Just crazy,' Gunzel said.

Georgina smiled again. She lit a cigarette. 'Once in Detroit we had to wait four hours for a flight. Engine trouble,' she said. 'I'd decided I wouldn't go at all just as they called the flight.'

I

Gunzel fidgeted with her handbag and watched Melek out of the corner of her eye.

'But I went along,' Georgina said. 'What with a lover waiting at the other end.'

Georgina's eyebrows always remained perched near her hairline. When she smiled the corners of her lips lifted slightly and that curve, along with the eyebrows and the hard horizontal of her green eyes, made an arabesque which reminded Maddy vaguely of the Blue Mosque: something about the strictness of the design coupled with the flowing lines. Then the face Maddy looked at dropped again into its frozen aspect.

Gunzel thought about Georgina's waiting lover. Then she thought about the airport in Izmir, where they were all going: the dryness, the scraggy palm trees, the shabby town bus with its dusty seats. 'Waiting drives me just crazy,' she repeated.

She went over to the information desk again and said something to the clerk. He looked at the clock and said something back to her without putting down his pencil. She came over to Georgina and Maddy and said: 'He says they're almost ready now. Fifteen minutes and the flight will be announced.'

Georgina smiled faintly through her cigarette smoke.

Maddy sat down on the bench next to Melek and when Melek looked over at her, Maddy smiled and put her hands in her pockets. 'Melek's not worried, are you Melek?' Maddy said.

Melek laughed hoarsely. Maddy always made her laugh, even when she didn't say anything funny. Something about the tone made Melek laugh. It was always as though Maddy meant something she wasn't saying. She confused Melek and Melek always laughed when she was confused. 'I never worry,' Melek said. She handed Maddy some pistachios.

2

'Melek never worries, never ever worries,' Maddy said. 'How nice for Melek.'

Melek blushed, which she did almost without provocation. She lowered her head nearer the bag of pistachios. Maddy looked at her for a moment, smiling, and then sighed and looked straight ahead as though she had forgotten Melek. She cracked a pistachio nut between her teeth.

'Bored?' Georgina said.

'No,' Maddy said. 'Wildly excited.'

'You have no patience,' Georgina said. 'You'd never make a peasant.'

'Imagine his surprise,' Maddy said.

Gunzel opened her handbag and took out a scented handkerchief. She unfolded it, held it briefly under her nose, refolded it and put it away again. She looked at the clock. She thought of her mother. 'God,' she said. 'I'm going crazy.'

On the plane they drank warm lemonade and ate slices of brown cake. They arrived in Izmir in the early afternoon. Gunzel looked at the dusty bus, squinting against the glare. Melek stood with her hands stuffed into her cape and her face as bland as pudding.

'Well, get on, get on, girls,' Gunzel said, climbing into the bus.

Maddy looked at Georgina from the privacy of her sunglasses.

'What are you thinking about?' Georgina said.

Maddy smiled slightly.

The ride into town took half an hour. At the city terminal Gunzel ran around on her thin legs and her high heels organizing a taxi. Melek sat next to the driver. Occasionally she spoke to Gunzel, in Turkish, and giggled. Gunzel stared straight ahead. The taxi stopped at the Anadolu Palas Hotel.

'Come around six,' Gunzel said, as Maddy and Georgina crawled out. 'My mother's a wonderful cook. Prima!' She made kissing noises in the air but her eyes stayed huge and apprehensive.

The taxi drove away.

'Is anything wrong, Gunzel?' Melek said.

'No.'

'Why do you look that way then?'

'What way?' Gunzel said.

'The way you look.'

'Melek, if you can't talk sensibly, don't talk.'

Melek fell silent. The driver said something to her over his shoulder and she giggled.

Georgina came out of the bathroom in her slip and bra. Maddy was lying stretched out on the bed with her eyes closed. She opened them and looked at Georgina.

'The water's hot and there's lots of it, if you want a bath,' Georgina said.

'I've wondered all day what you'd say to me when we were finally alone,' Maddy said.

'Oh shut up.'

Maddy laughed.

'This mélange . . .' Georgina began.

'Malaise,' Maddy said. 'Malaise.'

Georgina thought about it. 'You're probably right,' she said.

She got her skirt out of the suitcase and shook the wrinkles out and put it on. She wriggled into a sweater.

'Let's go and have some tea. I need comforting.'

Maddy rolled over to the side of the bed and sat up. 'Your trouble is, you're always looking for comfort,' she said. 'What about the rest?'

'What rest?' Georgina said. She put on her lipstick without a mirror.

4

'Are you going to leave your hair down like that?' Maddy said.

'No. I'm going to put it up. Why?'

'It softens you, down. You look like a mermaid. Like the Lorelei. If you were to sing a little song, I'd probably be lured into shipwreck.'

Georgina stopped brushing her hair and looked at Maddy. 'Would you like that?' she said.

Maddy shrugged. 'Shipwreck is a positive thing.'

Georgina picked a few long hairs out of her brush. 'What do you think about Gunzel?' she said.

Maddy laughed.

'What's funny?' Georgina said.

'You are,' Maddy said. 'What do you care what I think about Gunzel?'

'I don't *care*, I don't really *care*. I'm just curious, that's all,' Georgina said.

Georgina came over and sat down on the end of Maddy's bed. She smiled at Maddy, her face making its familiar arabesque.

'Stop being disingenuous,' Maddy said. 'It doesn't suit you.'

Georgina shrugged and ran the brush through her long hair. Maddy made a little sketch with her finger on Georgina's cheek. Georgina stopped brushing and stared at the floor. Then she kissed the inside of Maddy's wrist, which was near her mouth. Maddy took Georgina's hand and kissed the palm. Georgina was very still, looking at the top of Maddy's head. Then she withdrew her hand.

'My nervous virgin,' Maddy said.

'I'm not nervous.'

'You are. Do you feel like you're on stage?'

'A little,' Georgina said. 'You're always watching me.'

'Oh no I'm not,' Maddy said. 'It's just that you always *feel* watched. The Eye of God perhaps.'

'Oh, for Jesus sake,' Georgina said.

She got up and put her brush down on the bureau. 'I don't know why I came,' she said to Maddy.

'Shall I tell you?'

'Get dressed, for God's sake. I'm dying for some tea.'

Maddy got up very slowly and stretching and yawning went into the bathroom and turned on the water in the handbasin.

Georgina sat down on her bed and tapped her fingers in a tattoo on her knee. She listened to the water running in the bathroom and then she listened to the random splashing about which followed. Maddy's suitcase lay open on the floor near the bed. Georgina picked a stocking out of the suitcase and looked at it as though it were a very long condom she'd found in the Ladies' Room.

While they waited for tea in the hotel dining room, a beggar woman stuck a child with crusted eyes and black feet through the window next to their table. The small cankerous feet dangled just above the white teacloth like a macabre decoration. At the same moment the woman struck up her money chant: it was a single rhythm and very quick, so that rejection could not be pushed into any gaps between the words.

'Have you ever seen anything so dirty?' Georgina said. 'Look at those feet! I thought I'd seen some poor people in Michigan.'

'So now you know you haven't seen any poor people,' Maddy said. She dropped a lira coin into the woman's outstretched hand. 'It's like the rest of your experience: a little ersatz.'

'Why are you bent on insulting me?' Georgina said. 'That's an interesting question.' She watched the small black feet disappear through the window again.

'It's not an interesting question to anybody but you,'

Maddy said.

'Why . . . that's what I want to know. Gratuitously insulting.'

'Nothing gratuitous about it,' Maddy said. 'You've earned every insult.'

The waiter brought the tea in a silver pot. Maddy peered into the pot. 'No flies. No foreign matter visible. A lucky day again.'

'If you dislike me so, why do you want me?' Georgina said. 'That's interesting.'

Maddy poured the tea and dropped in the sugar. 'I'm maddened by your flesh,' she said. 'Your body drives me to the brink. And then those Hebraic eyes.'

Georgina sipped her tea and looked out the window towards the corniche. 'What's the time?' she said.

'It's remarkable,' Georgina said. 'It's really remarkable, the women in this country. Think of our own mothers behaving like that . . .'

'If you want to think of your own mother, that's your business,' Maddy said.

They were on the balcony, surrounded by house plants taking the evening air. Georgina stroked the leaves of a rubber plant. 'Where's Melek?' she said.

'In the kitchen, with Mama. And Gunzel's in the john, weeping I think.'

'Christ,' Georgina said. 'It's not as though anything happened. It was a lovely dinner.'

'A mother who won't eat with infidels and who's practically in purdah can be very upsetting to an emancipated woman like Gunzel,' Maddy said.

Georgina meditated. 'Do you think we should go?'

Maddy studied her over the rubber plant. 'A long evening alone in the Anadolu Palas,' she said. 'Think of that.'

'I'm not afraid of you,' Georgina said. 'If that's what you mean.'

'You're not?'

'No,' Georgina said. 'Not at all. Maybe in the beginning, but not now.'

'In the beginning of what?' Maddy said.

'In the beginning,' Georgina said. 'When we first met.'

'Oh,' Maddy said.

'Girls! Are you out there?' Gunzel shouted from inside. They came in. Gunzel had a blotchy face and was red in the eye. Her scented handkerchief leaked from her fist. She looked at them speechlessly, shaking her head from side to side and making guppy shapes with her mouth. Georgina walked over and embraced her efficiently. 'Don't give the whole thing a second thought,' she said. She lit a cigarette and looked across at Maddy. 'We certainly don't take any offence.'

'Girls, I can't tell you how she embarrasses me, I can't tell you,' Gunzel said. 'Mohammed was the worst thing that ever happened to her.'

'If she's happy with him . . .' Maddy said.

Gunzel clutched Maddy's sleeve and leaned her head against Maddy's shoulder. 'I wish there was something I could say! I never thought . . . with my good friends!'

Georgina exhaled a column of smoke through her nostrils and came over and patted Gunzel on the shoulder. 'We don't think any the worse of you for it,' she said. 'Now really, Gunzel, we must be going. Early start tomorrow, you know.'

Gunzel looked at Georgina, stricken. 'You are angry!' she said. 'I can see that you are angry with me. Oh God, what shall I do! It's all spoiled, spoiled!'

'No, Gunzel, not at all, Gunzel, not . . .'

'All this whole lovely trip, spoiled!' Gunzel clutched Maddy's arm even tighter, searching Maddy's face des-

8

perately, her nose a few inches away. 'Tell me you forgive me, Maddy. Tell me that,' she said.

'I forgive you, Gunzel,' Maddy said. 'I forgive you, although there's nothing to forgive.'

Gunzel wept, clinging to Maddy's arm. Georgina crossed the room and put her cigarette out. She came back and stood in front of Maddy with the corners of her mouth pulled down and her eyebrows even nearer her hairline than usual. 'We really must be going,' she said to Maddy. 'Mustn't we?'

Maddy disengaged herself from Gunzel. 'We must,' she said. 'Truly, we must.' She patted Gunzel's arm. 'Really, there's nothing to be upset about, Gunzel. Nothing at all. You can't really expect your mother to change her religion for dinner guests. We'll see you tomorrow.'

'Say goodbye to Melek for us, will you?' Georgina said. She picked her coat off the hook in the entrance hall.

Downstairs she looked at Maddy and said: 'Jesus, that's really disgusting.'

'What's disgusting?' Maddy said. 'Do you have any idea what you're referring to?'

'The whole thing. The whole thing's disgusting.'

'You mean,' Maddy said, 'a feeling of disgust in the air? Or do you want to be more specific?'

Georgina glared at her. 'You make me sick,' she said.

'Me? What have I done?'

'You . . .'

'Yes . . .?'

'Oh, never mind!'

Maddy laughed.

Georgina brooded. 'You never discourage her,' she said.

'Discourage her from what?' Maddy said.

'From pawing you, clutching at you and all that.'

'I should discourage a human being in need?' Maddy said. 'How do I know that clutching isn't salvation?'

'You're a sophist,' Georgina said.

'And what are you?'

Georgina stopped walking. 'I'm tired, that's what I am. Let's take a taxi, for God's sake.'

'And you didn't have to stare at me like that all the way to the hotel,' Georgina said. 'You didn't have to do that. The driver noticed.'

'Of course he did,' Maddy said. 'He always notices the subtlest changes in facial expression of all his passengers. He makes it his business to. It's part of his general examination for a licence.'

'Well, anyway . . .' Georgina said.

Maddy threw her skirt across a chair and went into the bathroom. She ran the water and came out again rubbing cream into her hands. She looked at Georgina. 'You are a ridiculous woman,' she said. 'It's humiliating to me that the sight of you unhinges me completely. Our relationship is concrete proof that Love is Blind.' She sat down on the bed and took her shoes off. 'You're a brainwashed little ninny.'

'Brainwashed!'

'Brainwashed,' Maddy said. 'You've been conditioned to salivate at the sound of men.'

'Listen, you smart bitch . . .'

'What you'd really like to do is play around with me for a couple of winters and marry a rising young Jewish lawyer in the spring. Only you can't figure out how to keep me around all that time without letting me into your precious bed, your Holy of Holies. And that idea makes you break out in a cold sweat, what with the eye of Yahweh and all. Yahweh in this case having become totally socialized.'

'Jeeesus . . .!' Georgina said. She threw her blouse across the room. It fell languidly on to the floor near her suitcase. 'You are the most insulting bitch . . .'

'It's only fair to tell you,' Maddy said, 'that I am not a faint Platonic type. Adoring from a distance I gave up when I was sixteen. I've never looked back.'

Georgina made small grunting sounds as though her words were running in several directions at once, like little wild panting pigs. Then she sat down on her bed and tears began falling down her cheeks in abundance.

'On the other hand,' Maddy said, 'you'd really like to go to bed with me, if you could only be somewhere else at the time.'

Maddy finished her third piece of brown bread and honey, wiped her fingers on the linen napkin and lit a cigarette. She settled back comfortably in her chair and gazed over Georgina's head at the bunting hanging across the face of the Iz Bank on the other side of the street. Georgina poured another cup of tea from the silver pot.

'We'll never get a place we can see from in this mob,' Georgina said. 'We should have got up in the middle of the night.'

'In the middle of the night, you were in no condition,' Maddy said. 'We're going to watch the parade from the roof of the hotel. I've already spoken to the manager.'

'From the roof . . .?' Georgina said.

'He said there's a lovely view from the roof. I thought you'd like a lovely view. All those lovely men in uniform. They even have boys in uniform, all very strong-limbed and doughty. You'll like that.'

'You're insufferable.'

''You've got that wrong,' Maddy said. 'You're insufferable. I'm suffering. But gracefully, so you'd hardly notice.'

'When does it start?' Georgina said.

'At noon,' Maddy said. She looked at her watch. 'Anytime you're ready, we can go up to the roof. There'll be others up there too. It's common practice, it seems, for the privileged residents of the hotel and other worldly people in the city to view parades and such things from the roof of the Anadolu Palas. Maybe you'll meet someone interesting up there, you never can tell. Just because you didn't get on very well with Osman Bey . . .'

'Get off Osman Bey,' Georgina said.

'I just didn't want you to feel defeated or discouraged because Osman Bey didn't work out,' Maddy said.

'I wasn't interested in Osman Bey, for God's sake!'

'You weren't? I'm delighted to hear that. I thought for a while you were interested in Osman Bey. Oh well, that's a different thing altogether then, isn't it?'

Georgina swallowed her cold tea and stood up. 'One of these days, Maddy,' she said, 'you're going to go too far.'

'I've already been too far,' Maddy said. 'And you're too short to threaten tall women.'

Maddy hung over the railing to watch a khaki tank crawl by. There was another Bauhaus man projecting out of the open trap. Several columns of uniformed men followed, chests billowing out like flags in the wind. Two soldiers in front bore aloft a twelve-foot banner of Atatürk, shrewd eyes six feet across.

Gunzel spindled her way through the crowd, smiling nervously. She grasped Maddy's arm. 'You're not angry about last night?' she said.

'Not at all, not a particle,' Maddy said.

'I couldn't bear it,' Gunzel said.

Maddy touched her shoulder and smiled reassuringly.

'Absolutely nothing to worry about,' she said. 'Just forget about it.'

Gunzel smiled tremulously. 'You're very understanding,' she said.

'Very,' Maddy said.

'Are you having a good time?' She cast quick glances around the roof.

'It couldn't be a nicer day for a parade,' Maddy said. 'It's like a parody of a parade day.'

Gunzel fidgeted, plucking at her collar and shifting from one high-heeled crocodile shoe to the other. 'Where's Georgina?' she said.

Maddy motioned to her left. Gunzel swivelled to see Georgina standing a bit farther down the roof talking to a very tall eagle-beaked Turk. One of her hips was pushed languidly forward and she was gesticulating prettily with her cigarette. Gunzel looked at her for a moment and then turned back to Maddy. 'Have you made any plans for this evening?' she said.

Maddy shrugged. 'We are improvising at the moment.'

'Perhaps you'd like to go out to the Park. It's a lovely park. There's a lake there, with swans.'

'It sounds nice,' Maddy said. 'But I'll have to ask Georgina. She may have something else in mind.'

'We wouldn't have to stay all evening in the Park,' Gunzel said. 'We could go to a club, if you wanted to. My brother would be pleased to take us.'

Maddy nodded and smiled. She watched Georgina lean forward towards the eagle-beaked Turk, laughing, her breasts shaking under her sweater. 'Would it be all right if I rang you up later and let you know about the Park?' she said.

'Oh fine,' Gunzel said. 'That would be fine.'

In the middle of a sweep with her cigarette Georgina noticed Gunzel. The oblique eyes went Mongolian. She

13

pushed through the crowd, holding her cigarette in front of her like a beacon.

'Hello there!' Georgina said. 'I never dreamt you still watched parades, Gunzel. I mean, you must have seen so many of them . . .'

Tall young Eagle-Beak was just behind her, wearing a slightly abstract smile which was not directed to anyone but could be used in an emergency.

Georgina made a little hiatus in the circle of three and gestured at Eagle-Beak over her shoulder. 'This is Haluk Ersan,' she said. 'Madelaine Tilson and Gunzel Vedin.'

Haluk Bey lowered his heavy eyelids and the smile became briefly definite and directed. Gunzel stared at him coldly. He ignored her.

'I must be off now, girls,' Gunzel said. 'Have a good time. Ring me later. You've got my number.'

'You bet,' Georgina said. She watched Gunzel go. She waved at her when she reached the door leading off the roof. She looked at Maddy for a moment silently. 'I suppose you've made plans for us which include Gunzel,' she said.

'Not necessarily,' Maddy said. 'That will depend.'

'On what?'

Haluk Bey gazed across the rooftops of the city with a preoccupied air.

'Haluk has invited us to the casino this evening,' Georgina said.

'Has he?' Maddy said. She leaned back against the railing and looked up at the bottom of Haluk Bey's chin.

'He's expecting a friend of his any moment,' Georgina said. 'He assures me this friend is an especially nice person.' She smiled archly up at Haluk Bey. 'Isn't that what you said, Haluk?'

'That's right,' he said. 'Hasan is a very nice person. He has travelled, he is a man of the world.' A whisper of sarcasm in his voice made Maddy desert Georgina's face. Haluk Bey continued to survey the rooftops in front of him.

'That's very important of course,' Maddy said. 'Being a man of the world is of the very first importance, like white teeth.'

Georgina looked uncomfortable. 'Do you want to go, or not?' she said.

'How do I know until I've met this very nice man of the world?' Maddy said. 'He could have two heads and still travel.'

Haluk Bey laughed. 'She's a very sensible lady,' he said to Georgina. 'Like all American ladies I've met.' He had a very languorous voice, as though he were rich and it had never been necessary to hurry.

Georgina smiled at him and took out a cigarette, which he lit for her in an offhand way without the usual Turkish flourish. 'Undoubtedly, you smoke too much,' he said. 'You will ruin your pretty self.'

Hasan Bey appeared on the roof. He was shorter than Eagle-Beak. His hair was beginning to recede and his jowls to thicken. His heavy eyelids drooped over his eyes but not enough to conceal the avidity. He smiled intimately at the world. He came over, holding his hand out for Haluk Bey, while he looked over the females. He bowed. He cupped his hand immediately around Maddy's elbow. 'French?' he said. 'You look very French. No? But you must have some French blood in your family . . .'

'I don't think it bears looking into,' Maddy said.

'Let's have a drink somewhere,' Haluk Bey said. 'The sun makes a thirst.'

'What do you think of Hasan?' Georgina said.

Maddy was stretched out in a crucifix position on the

15

bed, studying the ceiling. 'He's rudimentary,' she said. 'Perhaps inchoate is the word I want.'

Georgina stopped filing her thumbnail. 'What's wrong with him?' she said.

'I just told you,' Maddy said. 'God, I'm tired. Brandy and rudimentary people make a fatiguing combination. Only the brandy goes to your head.' She sat up and looked at Georgina. 'I gather you and Haluk Bey hit it off superbly. He even forgot to be bitter now and again.'

'He had an unfortunate affair with an American girl when he was over there studying,' Georgina said. 'They were engaged and she jilted him at the last moment.'

'Really,' Maddy said. 'So now we've all got to convince him we're okay, harmless and sweet-intentioned.'

'You're hard-hearted,' Georgina said.

'Does he feel he's got a licence to be rude to us all because his heart was broken by a fellow-national?'

Georgina walked into the bathroom and began running a bath.

'He's just rude enough to appeal to a potentially servile female like you,' Maddy yelled over the running water. 'I wonder how both of us could have been belched out by the same X-chromosome.'

Georgina came back into the room in her bathrobe. She lit a cigarette and sat down on her bed.

'Do you know,' Maddy said, 'that Hasan Bey has got an album of photographs of the women in his life? Women in his life in this case meaning anybody he could hold still long enough for the flashbulb to go off. He told me about his collection. He said how he was looking forward to adding me to his album. Tonight at the casino.'

Georgina was silent, smoking.

'He's going to show me the album sometime before we leave,' Maddy said. 'He insists. It's as though he's not really a lady-killer unless I see the ladies he's killed.'

Georgina got up and put her cigarette out. 'It's not as though you're going to marry him,' she said. 'It's just one night at the casino.'

Maddy stretched her arms up towards the ceiling and yawned. 'One night with Hasan Bey may be the equivalent of a lobotomy. Don't be all night in the bathtub.'

When they got to the Lake Casino the Italian band, all in snow-white suits and fuzzy-skinned white shoes, was just in the middle of a brassy version of 'Volare'. Hasan Bey smiled happily, snapped his fingers and did a couple of twirls around Maddy as they stood in the foyer.

'One of my favourite numbers,' he said. 'Let us dance.'

'I'd like to check my coat first,' Maddy said. 'I never like to dance with my coat on. It inhibits me.'

He stared at her a moment. Then he said: 'You have a very marvellous sense of humour.'

They followed the waiter to their table, which was near the ice-cream orchestra all jumping up and down on their spongy soles. The whole band seemed to be moving in random patterns around the bandstand.

Georgina and Haluk Bey trailed along behind. Haluk Bey seemed dispirited and wore his sardonic smile. He kept directing this smile at Georgina, who ignored it. She swept ahead to their table with her face fixed in its most impervious mask and her eyebrows tirelessly at her hairline. She was wearing a red serape from Mexico and when she sat down one end of it dropped on to the floor, where Haluk trod it underfoot. She dragged it up and glared at him icily.

'I beg your pardon,' Haluk Bey said and smiled his bitter smile at her. Before she could forgive him, he turned to the wine steward.

'Now that you've got rid of your coat, let us dance,'

17

Hasan Bey said to Maddy, snapping his fingers happily. He leaned over towards her confidentially. 'I think you must be a very wonderful dancer.'

Maddy rose and accompanied Hasan Bey to the floor. While 'Volare' pumped through her skull like a nail, she sniffed Hasan Bey's aromatic ear and watched – when she was turned in the right direction – Georgina and Haluk Bey. Georgina was talking animatedly, smoke pouring out of her nostrils. Haluk Bey appeared receptive to the animation. At one point he even dropped his arm across the back of her chair. On the next whirl around they were both silent. Georgina was watching the trumpet soloist with a bored expression. Haluk Bey was emptying a glass.

'You are a very marvellous dancer, so light on your feet,' Hasan Bey said. He held her chair for her. He lit a cigarette and passed it to her, his eyes moist with seduction. 'I shall always remember our first dance together,' he said.

'It *was* memorable,' Maddy said. Haluk Bey laughed.

'What's funny?' Georgina said to him.

'Nothing,' he said. 'Do you want to dance?'

'How could I resist an invitation like that?' Georgina said.

Haluk Bey stood up. 'Exactly,' he said. They proceeded to the floor.

Hasan Bey poured Maddy a glass of champagne and filled his own glass. His eyes darted around the room like a ferret sniffing out a rabbit. He's looking for the photographer, Maddy thought. God. I am being collected. Who will see me in the future, lying prone in Hasan Bey's album?

'We shall eat now,' Hasan Bey said. 'A very nice antipasto to begin.'

'That's a good idea,' Maddy said. She drank her

champagne and watched Haluk Bey spin Georgina around the floor. He kept looking over his shoulder at the band and smiling at the saxophonist, whom he apparently knew. Georgina's face was frozen. Maddy looked at her watch. They had not yet been in the casino for an hour.

'And then,' Hasan Bey said, 'I worked for NATO for a while, a year or two. I made many American friends during this period.'

He waved frantically at the wandering photographer who had just finished blowing off his flashbulb in the face of a nearby couple. 'I have many American friends,' he repeated. 'Next to the French girls, I like best the American girls.'

'Really?' Maddy said. She refilled her glass. She looked at Georgina standing rigidly in the middle of the dance floor while the band deliberated cacophonously on the next number. Haluk Bey had gone over to have a chat with the saxophonist.

'Smile,' Hasan Bey whispered in her ear, putting his arm around her shoulders and beaming up at the photographer on the other side of the champagne bottle standing in its ice. Maddy arranged her face to resemble as nearly as possible the face of a captive woman in the arms of an amorous S.S. man and stared at the camera. The bulb exploded and she felt Hasan Bey go limp next to her as though he had been shot or just released from an iron maiden. 'Ah,' he said. He jumped up to order his prints from the photograher. He smiled at him, embraced him slightly, patted his shoulder and offered him a drink. When the interlude was over, he returned to the table and refilled the glasses.

'What about that very nice antipasto to begin?' Maddy said.

'Ah,' Hasan Bey said again. He ordered a menu, which

he studied conscientiously. The band had decided on a rhumba but Haluk Bey appeared to be foxtrotting to it. Georgina's face was stony. On the last note she dropped her arms and walked stiffly back to the table without looking around or speaking to Haluk Bey. She sat down across from Maddy.

'I need some of that,' she said, pushing her glass towards Maddy.

'Allow me,' Hasan Bey said, putting the menu down for a moment.

'We're on the point of eating some very nice antipasto to begin,' Maddy said.

Georgina grimaced. 'Do you need to go to the powder room?'

'It just so happens,' Maddy said, getting up. Haluk Bey had stopped to say something to a young man two tables away. Maddy and Georgina threaded their way to the powder room.

Once inside, Georgina looked at Maddy desperately and slumped down on to a little velveteen-covered stool in front of a mirror. 'For chrissakes, I can't go through with this,' she said. 'Such a bore, I can't tell you. Such a . . . such a . . .' She staggered into unintelligibility and a few tears dribbled down her cheeks. 'You wouldn't believe some of the things he's said to me.'

'Don't worry,' Maddy said. 'I'll get you out. Now listen, as soon as we finish the antipasto, I'll say that I have a splitting headache and want to go back to the hotel. You will say that you must accompany me, since you know how bad these migraine things get and I mustn't be left alone. Then we'll go. And if the Beys don't feel like taking us back, we'll get a taxi. Finished. How's that?'

'Great,' Georgina said, wiping her eyes. She pressed some powder onto her shiny cheeks. 'Jesus . . . that Haluk Bey.'

They returned to the table, faces inscrutable, secure in their foreknowledge of events. Haluk Bey was sprawled in his chair glowering at the tablecloth. Hasan Bey twirled the gold ring on his left hand and stared vacuously into the thick half-light of the casino. Hasan Bey stood up and waved Maddy through to her seat. Haluk Bey remained sprawled in his chair. He looked up at Georgina with melancholy eyes.

'We are having a wonderful Circassian chicken,' Hasan Bey said. 'The antipasto comes at any moment.'

Georgina folded her hands prayerfully under her chin and leaned forward on her elbows, her eyes as inaccessible as a conch in its shell. Haluk Bey straightened up and looked at her profile with intense though saddened concentration. Then he leaned over and encircled her wrists with one of his hands. Georgina turned and looked at him as though he were a purse-snatcher. He looked back at her meltingly, a small rueful smile on his lips. He got up and very gently led Georgina to the dance floor. The ice-cream men were being very restrained and playing a ballad. Haluk Bey pressed Georgina's cheek against his breast, embraced her tightly and moved her liquidly across the floor. Georgina was astonished but her face had no way left to reflect this condition, considering the usual position of her eyebrows and the customary brightness of her oblique green eyes.

Maddy ate an olive off the antipasto tray and watched Haluk Bey smiling mournfully into Georgina's face.

'Christ,' she said.

'Is there anything wrong with your olive?' Hasan Bey said.

'I was meditating on the place of vanity in captivity.'

'Pardon?' Hasan Bey said. His mouth was full of salami.

'Forget it,' she said. 'Be good enough to pass me an anchovy.'

Georgina returned to the table smiling beatifically like a Perugino Virgin, as though harbouring a precious secret. Haluk Bey was all tender solicitude. He arranged a selection of antipasto and set it delicately before her. Georgina picked at it as though in a dream, talking to Haluk in small murmurs between mouthfuls.

'Let's dance,' Maddy said to Hasan Bey. 'Swallow all that stuff in your mouth and let's dance.'

Hasan Bey looked at her astonished and then wiped his fingers and smiled. 'You have a wonderful, very wonderful sense of humour,' he said.

By the time they got back to the table after a vigorous samba, Georgina was stony-faced again, her lips squeezed tightly together as though she were suppressing tears. Haluk Bey was slumped down in his chair, pressing circles into the tablecloth with his champagne glass.

'I've got a terrible headache,' Maddy said loudly. 'I must go back to the hotel. Immediately.'

Hasan Bey looked at her incredulously. 'Headache?' he said. 'But on the dance floor –'

'I have a wonderful way of concealing my pain,' she said. 'But the mask is slipping away from me. I really do have to go, before the attack becomes any worse.' She paused. 'It could become a great deal worse. It could render me incapable.'

'Oh . . .' Hasan Bey said.

Georgina looked at Maddy with her lips pressed together tightly and said nothing.

'If it gets too bad, I'll have to call a doctor,' Maddy said. 'Isn't that right, Georgina?'

'What?' she said.

'I said: I may have to call a doctor. For the migraine.'

'Oh,' Georgina said. She wedged a sip of champagne between her pressed lips. She brandished a tissue vaguely around her eyes.

'I am very sad to hear that,' Hasan Bey said. 'I will take you to my apartment and give you some medication for headaches which I have. It is very wonderful medication.'

'I want to go back to the hotel,' Maddy said. 'Immediately.'

'I will take you,' Hasan Bey said, standing up. 'You will excuse us?' he said to Georgina and Haluk Bey. Haluk Bey looked up and nodded, preoccupied. Georgina kept her glazed eyes fixed on the antipasto tray.

Hasan Bey's apartment was in Teutonic Modern. A radio-phonograph in a bulbous contoured cabinet with chromium buttons undulated eight feet across one side of his sitting room. Through the open bedroom door Maddy caught a glimpse of a swollen wardrobe with bright brass knobs. Hasan Bey put on a Sinatra record, which he had acquired through his NATO friends of earlier years. 'A Foggy Day in London Town' rumbled out of six speakers, penetrated Maddy's abdomen and rose singingly to her ears by way of her throat. Hasan Bey ushered her to a soft chair where she sat throbbing with the bass tones, her feet ankle-deep in a thick orange carpet, while he disappeared to search out his headache medication. The pain in Maddy's head was now authentic and she was so heavy with wrath that the weight of it made her ache rheumatically. There was a hard knot of murder in her breast. It was looking for a home. One wrong word from Hasan Bey and it would shoot through his heart like a spike. She would leave him impaled on his damask sofa like a light-olive butterfly, the droop of his eyelids total.

He returned. He carried a lemon-coloured vial in his right hand. His left hand lay lissomely in the pocket of the maroon silk dressing-gown with black shawl collar

23

which he was now wearing.

'I see you just slipped into something more comfortable,' Maddy said. Her eyes felt like two orange balloons. She squinted around them.

He beamed, all of his long white teeth gleaming unnaturally. 'Do you like my apartment?' he said. 'I like very modern furnishings. I do not like Turkish carpets.'

'You have succeeded in creating an environment in which any Turkish carpet would be ashamed to lie,' she said.

He paused a moment, considering the nuances of his translation and then smiled happily. He poured a tumbler of scotch and shook out two tablets into her palm. 'You will feel very wonderful in a minute,' he said. 'This is a marvellous medication for headaches.'

She swallowed the tablets, knowing they would be the end of her and that sometime that night, in the dusty corridors of the Anadolu Palas, a chambermaid would find her body stretched full-length, nose down, and thoroughly dead. Post-mortem would reveal champagne, scotch, and two mysterious tablets lying in the sac of her stomach, right alongside three anchovies and two stuffed olives.

'Haven't you got anything to eat here?' she said. 'If I feed the pain maybe it will give up and go away.'

'To eat . . .?' Hasan Bey looked puzzled.

'Yes. To eat. Food. Haven't you got a kitchen? Didn't you work for NATO long enough to order some kind of kitchen from Bremerhaven?'

'Bremerhaven . . .?' Hasan Bey said uncertainly.

'Yes! Bremerhaven! Food! Bread and butter. Milk. Anything. Haven't you got a goat somewhere with dripping tits?' she shouted.

He looked at her as though he had suddenly forgotten all his English. Sinatra was booming out 'Stairway to the

24

Stars' through his six speakers. Hasan Bey clutched the sash of his dressing-gown for security.

"Goat . . .' he finally said. 'I have got no goat.'

'Then for God's sake why did you invite me here?' Maddy yelled. The yell shook something loose inside her skull. It crossed her mind quickly that it was probably a central artery. She moaned and gripped her head, rocking from side to side like an old peasant woman whose son had fallen in battle. Hasan Bey moved nervously forward and put his hand out imploringly.

'Do not become sick,' he said. 'I beg you.'

She looked up through her fingers. 'I am already sick. I am on the point of death. That is fact.'

Hasan Bey smiled wanly. 'You are playing,' he said. 'You must not play like that with Hasan. That is very naughty.'

Maddy slumped back in her chair, feeling the thump of Sinatra's bass player in her kidneys. 'Listen, Hasan . . . do you think you could turn off that music? Do you think anything like silence is possible in your apartment?'

'You do not like the music? That's very strange. All the American girls I have known have liked Frank Sinatra.'

'I have nothing personal against Frank Sinatra, you understand,' she said. 'But if you don't turn off that music in exactly sixty seconds my head is going to blow up right in front of your eyes. Pieces of it will be everywhere, all over your modern furnishings. How will that look?'

Hasan Bey looked around the room, trying to visualize it. 'I think you are making a joke,' he said.

'You've got thirty seconds to find out,' Maddy said.

Hasan Bey went over and switched off one of the knobs under the long row of chromed s's that serpentined across the eight feet of teak veneer. The sudden silence was overwhelming. Maddy felt faint. She closed her eyes.

'Haven't you even got a carrot?' she whispered. She opened her eyes and looked at him. 'What do you do for food around here . . . go next door with a begging bowl? Hang around cafés waiting for the pilaf to be flung out?'

Hasan Bey sucked the tassels of his dressing-gown sash and looked at her apprehensively. His mainspring had snapped. Maddy could hear no ticking from his chest. He turned and went out of the room and returned immediately with his satin-covered photograph album. It was all he had left, now that Sinatra had gone. He sat down on the edge of the sofa and opened the album. He leaned out across the space between the sofa and Maddy's chair, holding the album towards her like a sacrificial offering, nodding encouragingly, smiling transient little smiles.

'This one is French. The photograph was made ten years ago. You see I had a moustache then.' He turned the album around and studied the photograph. 'Perhaps it is better with a moustache.' He shrugged and turned the album towards Maddy again. He flipped over the page and recited: 'This was a very wonderful American girl. Very blonde. Her name was Nancy. Very wonderful girl.' His arms were tiring. He balanced the album on his knees and turned the page. 'This one –' he began.

Maddy was silent. She sat with her arms hanging over the sides of the chair. She looked at Hasan Bey from a great distance. She gazed at his pink scalp from Mount Sinai. She was impassive. Even the murder had passed away. She no longer wanted a carrot. Hasan Bey marched doggedly on through the album, not looking up at her any more. Sweat glistened in his eyebrows.

'This one was French also. She had very marvellous eyes. Oh la la . . . she had . . .' He put the album tenderly down on the sofa next to him and stood up. 'Perhaps you would not mind if I put on some Latin music, very low. Perhaps that would not disturb you?' he said.

His voice seemed to reach her from a neighbouring country, crossing the Aegean under water in a thin pipe. She nodded. He plucked a record out of its cover and dropped it into the smooth guts of the machine. He carefully turned the volume down. As soon as the rhumba began, Maddy could dimly hear the ticking in his chest resume. He came back to the sofa and picked up the album. He turned a page.

'Now this one,' he said, 'this one –'

A moan was heard. Hasan Bey looked up, startled. He stared at Maddy. 'Did you speak?' he said.

She shook her head weakly.

He looked at her tenderly. He laid the album on the sofa again, open at his place. 'Rhumba!' he said. 'My favourite.' He grasped Maddy's arm and pulled her forward.

She laughed grotesquely. The sound seemed to come out of one side of her mouth and one nostril, it was distorted, it had lived in unspeakable places. It grew in intensity. Hasan Bey stood transfixed, his extended hand frozen where it hung. He moved back two steps. Maddy stood up, laughing wildly. Tears began to emerge from her painful eyes. She bent forward, breathless. She spluttered, looking for oxygen. Then she coughed once asthmatically and was silent. The rhumba was displaced by a tango. Hasan Bey watched for a moment to be sure the paroxysm was finished. Then he walked over and put one arm around her shoulders and one hand squarely on a breast. His eyes gleamed liquidly under their fleshy folds. 'My darling . . .' he murmured. 'Sweetling . . .' he breathed heavily into Maddy's ear. 'You are the girl of my dreams.'

Maddy seized the hand hovering around her navel. 'Goats,' she croaked into Hasan Bey's face.

The face recoiled a few inches. 'You said . . .?'

'Goats, I said. Only a goat will do. We all have our skeletons in the closet.' She reversed from the hand and the arm. Hasan Bey encircled air briefly. She leaned against the venetian blinds with a sad tremulous brave smile, like Mrs Miniver standing in a doorway saying farewell.

'Only a goat . . . will do,' she whispered. She blinked. She lowered her eyes and turned to half-profile. 'An incident in early childhood,' she said. 'You understand.'

'But a goat . . .' he waved frantically, 'a goat cannot give you what I can give you!'

Maddy allowed a small sob to escape her trembling lips. 'Ah . . .' she said. 'I know, I know.'

Hasan Bey flung open his maroon silk dressing-gown. 'Have you ever seen such a goat as this!' he shouted. 'I must ask you to be honest.'

'No,' she said quietly. 'I must admit . . . no goat of my acquaintance . . .'

'Sweetling . . .' he murmured hoarsely. 'Come with me. I shall put to shame every goat you have known in your life.'

She looked at him with intense luminous melancholy. 'One's destiny,' she breathed softly, 'cannot be resisted. One must have the courage of one's perversities. Dear Hasan Bey . . . put your goat away. It is all quite, quite useless.'

'Tomorrow,' he said passionately. 'In two days, in three. We can practise!'

'Ah . . .' she smiled bitterly. 'How many times have I heard those fateful words – We Can Practise. And how many aching disappointments have filled my breast, how many times my heart has broken like a dry twig.'

Hasan Bey sank down on to the sofa, groping for his photograph album. A samba took over the six speakers, the marimbas rattling away in the silence. Maddy sighed deeply and slipped into her coat. 'I must go,' she said. 'I am fatigued with frustration.'

Hasan Bey raised his weighty lids and looked at her, his mouth a slack circle of pain. Then his jaws snapped shut with decision. 'Do not despair, sweetling,' he said huskily. 'We will find a solution to this problem. A very wonderful solution,' he added.

When Georgina came back to the Anadolu Palas at 2 a.m. Maddy was lying awake in her bed, stiff and incandescent with rage.

'Put on all the lights,' Maddy said. 'I want to see your Judas face clearly.'

The light went on. Georgina stood uncertainly by the door. Then she shrugged and dropped her serape over the chair. 'I might have guessed you'd be unreasonable,' she said. She kicked her shoes off and sat down on the foot of the bed.

'Unreasonable!' Maddy said. She sat bolt upright in her bed. 'Unreasonable!' she repeated. 'Do you know where I was until 1 a.m.?'

Georgina massaged her toes, gazing blankly at the faded carpet. 'Where?' she said, warily.

'With that lunatic Hasan Bey, that's where,' Maddy said. 'First in his very wonderful apartment. Then in a taxi for a couple of hours. I think we came home by way of Greece.'

Georgina was silent for a moment, pulling her toes apart and letting them snap together again under her stocking. 'Well, I'm sorry,' she said defensively. 'I'm just sorry, that's all I can say.'

'Is that all you can say?' Maddy said very quietly. 'Is that really all you can say, you perfidious wretch?'

'Now, listen . . .' Georgina began. 'I know we were

29

supposed to leave the casino together, but I just couldn't do it.'

'You just couldn't do it,' Maddy said.

'No.'

'Why not?'

Georgina leaned back on the bed. Maddy stared at the underside of her chin and waited.

'Haluk knew that we were planning to bolt,' Georgina said. 'He told me he knew he'd offended me and he couldn't blame me but he just couldn't control himself, not after that American affair. He said he'd felt different for the first time since coming back, with me. He said he thought he was beginning to get over it a little but that he still had these relapses, he couldn't help himself.'

'Relapses . . .' Maddy said. She lit a cigarette and pulled at a strand of hair behind her ear.

'He said he just couldn't stand it that he and I were going to turn out just like the other times, that it was going to be the same thing all over again. He asked me to be patient with him and to forgive him. He cried, you know.'

'He cried . . .' Maddy said, exhaling smoke with such force that her nostrils felt scorched.

'I couldn't do it to him,' Georgina said. 'I couldn't run out on him. I would have felt like such a terrible heel.'

'He needed you. You couldn't refuse to help him,' Maddy said.

'That's it exactly,' Georgina said. 'It would have been inhuman.' She sighed and sat up again, rubbing her neck, unbuttoning her blouse.

'Each female recapitulates the history of her sex,' Maddy said. 'You are an article of use, like a toilet roll.'

'I'm not going to sit here and be insulted by you again,' Georgina said. She got up and went into the bathroom and slammed the door.

Maddy rose from her bed and flung open the bath-room door. She glared at Georgina, standing at the hand-basin in her bra, who looked back at Maddy through the mirror.

'Do you know that Hasan Bey thinks I only do it with goats?' she said. 'Can you imagine that he actually believes this? Meditate on the intelligence that lies con-cealed behind those hooded eyes . . .' She slammed the door again. She went over and sat down on the side of her bed. She listened to the silence in the bathroom. Had Georgina fainted face-down over the open john? Maddy did not go and check on this possibility. She lit another cigarette and examined the wall.

In a moment the bathroom door opened very quietly and Georgina came out. She knelt by her suitcase and slipped a nightie – white with blue ribbons across the bosom and along the hem – over her head and wriggled out of her bra and panties underneath. Then she came over to Maddy's bed. Her hair was down, trailing over her shoulders, strands of it falling forward to nestle in the blue ribbons. She had arranged two little moist curls on her forehead. She looked like a decadent child waiting for a bedtime story.

'Maddy darling . . .' she said softly. 'I'm awfully sorry about this evening, I really am.' She sat down next to Maddy on the bed. She touched Maddy's shoulder gently and smiled. Maddy turned and looked at her. 'Don't be mad,' Georgina said.

'I have a really magnificently insane desire to kiss you all up and down your neck, but I won't do it,' Maddy said. 'I simply won't do it.'

Georgina delicately swept the hair away from her neck and leaned towards her. 'Why not?' she said.

'One of these days,' Maddy said, 'you're going to pre-sent your neck in that light-hearted manner of yours and

I'm going to take a devastating bite out of it and knock you unconscious and violate you and leave your naked ruined body in the corridors of some seedy hotel somewhere in the world.'

Georgina stared at her, startled, her mouth hanging open. 'I think there's something vicious about you,' she said. 'Really vicious.'

'Not vicious,' Maddy said. 'Not vicious. You're inept with the language. You're imprecise. Not vicious, sweetling. Violent. There is definitely something violent about me, vis-à-vis you. My theory is that the violence is provoked by the knowledge that I am infatuated with an artifact. That's my theory. I've given it a good deal of thought. Not that it matters in the least, not that having it all worked out will interfere in any way with my infatuation. Oh no . . . if you collected all Haluk Bey's old semen in a Dixie Cup and went to sleep sobbing over it every night, I'd still want to kiss you up and down your neck the next morning.' She gazed at Georgina sorrowfully. 'Your neck is the *Ding an Sich*,' she said.

'You know I don't know German,' Georgina said.

'It doesn't matter,' Maddy said. 'It's a private conversation.'

Georgina put her arm around Maddy's waist. 'Please don't be mad at me,' she said. She kissed Maddy's cheek. 'What are you thinking about?' she said.

'I am trying to resist the self-loathing that is so inappropriate to the modern personality,' she said.

Georgina went over and crawled into her bed. She smiled fondly at Maddy across the chasm between them.

'What makes you look so angelic tonight?' Maddy said. 'So beatific . . . is it because you've come through it all unscathed, the little virgin in her white nightie with the blue ribbons?'

'I'm *not* a virgin,' Georgina said.

'Of course you are.'

'Don't be so silly,' Georgina said. 'I'm twenty-five.'

'I'm going to put the light off now,' Maddy said. 'You can lie there and have sweet virginal dreams.'

She switched off the lamp and slipped down in the bed. She sighed, she prepared her head for sleep, she concentrated on a field of wheat but Georgina kept romping through it intermittently, blue ribbons flying.

'Maddy . . .?' Georgina said.

'What is it?'

She giggled. 'Does he really think you only do it with goats?'

Izmir was like a flat white body prostrate with sunstroke. She had palm trees on her wrists and ankles and a dull eye. The Bay of Izmir was cradled in her waist, bluer than lapis. A large yacht was anchored a little way offshore. It emitted no festive sounds. It was as subdued as the town, despite the thirtieth celebration of Turkish Independence. Some Greeks, Maddy thought, had left it there and rushed off to Athens. It was a decoy or an alibi. Nobody was home, nobody ever would be home.

She found Gunzel eating cheese börecks in the Park Pavilion overlooking the lake.

'I'm so hungry all the time,' Gunzel said, wiping her chin. 'I want just to eat from morning till night.' She giggled. 'It's my nerves I think.'

'What's wrong with your nerves?' Maddy said. She sat down across from Gunzel and looked out the long glass window towards the lake. Three swans were dousing their heads.

'I'm sorry Georgina couldn't come,' Gunzel said.

'Prior engagement,' Maddy said.

'With that Haluk Ersan?' Gunzel said. 'I hope she won't get involved with him.'

33

'Georgina doesn't get involved with people,' Maddy said. 'Is Haluk Bey notorious or something like that?'

Gunzel shrugged. 'Oh, I wouldn't say that . . .'

'Why shouldn't Georgina get involved with him then, assuming she could?'

Gunzel pushed böreck crumbs around her plate and cast up little dark nervous smiles at Maddy. 'He's not the kind of man Georgina should have something to do with. No. Not at all. His reputation . . .' She tapped her nails on the table and looked at Maddy coyly. 'With women,' she finished.

'Oh,' Maddy said. 'Do you think he'll try to rape her? Is that his game?'

'Oh no!' Gunzel looked alarmed. 'He wouldn't do that.'

'Then everything's all right,' Maddy said. 'Anything less than rape, Georgina doesn't notice.'

Gunzel looked uncertain. 'I don't understand you sometimes. I think the idiom . . .'

Maddy ordered a cognac and lit a cigarette. 'I am feeling rather blissful at this moment,' she said, leaning back in her chair. 'The sun's very nice.'

Gunzel bent forward anxiously. 'Sometimes I think you don't like Georgina very much. Sometimes you speak about her in a way . . .'

Maddy felt her bliss begin to slide away.

Gunzel played with her fork and looked out the window. 'The swans are very fine, aren't they?' she said.

'Gorgeous,' Maddy said. She swallowed half her cognac in a gulp. 'Where's Melek?' she said.

Gunzel twitched impatiently. 'Melek? Melek is here and there, here and there. Melek is not important.'

'Oh?'

'Melek is very unsatisfactory.'

'Is she?'

Gunzel leaned back in her chair and smiled at Maddy. 'Once,' she said, 'I had such a wonderful friend. Two years ago she left Turkey. Before then, we went everywhere together. We were never apart. She always understood what was in my heart before I spoke it.' She paused. 'Melek,' she said bitterly, 'Melek does not understand whether her head is pointing up or down. She understands nothing. She is unsatisfactory. She must be told everything.' She was silent, fuming with irritation.

'She's very young,' Maddy said. 'Perhaps your other friend was older and wiser than Melek. Perhaps she had more experience.'

Gunzel looked at her sadly. 'No,' she said hopelessly, 'Melek will never be anything but an idiot. I must say to her, Melek, come here . . . Melek, go there . . . do this . . . do that. She is dumb, like a sheep in the field. She will go back to her village and marry a man her mother has chosen for her and she will never regret anything.'

'But you will regret Melek?' Maddy said. She finished her cognac. 'You will regret her, isn't that so?' She motioned to the waiter to bring her another of the same.

Gunzel smiled gratefully. 'You see that, do you? You see why I would regret her? After my first friend . . .' She frowned. She fell silent for a moment. When the waiter set Maddy's second cognac on the table, Gunzel ordered an orange liqueur. 'Melek leaves a bitter taste in the mouth, after my first friend,' she said.

'Melek is very sweet,' Maddy said. 'Innocent and sweet. That's very rare.'

'She must be told everything!' Gunzel's voice was almost shrill. It seemed to surprise her. She smiled at Maddy nervously. 'You see, I grow impatient.'

'I see that,' Maddy said.

Gunzel considered, rotating her orange liqueur. 'Georgina doesn't have to be told everything,' she said. 'Does she?'

'Georgina can be told nothing. That's very different.'
Maddy was beginning to feel a little drunk. Two stiff
cognacs and a place in the warm sun were taking their
toll. In a moment her mind would wander away and
forget to return to Gunzel. Should she prevent that now,
while she still could? Or abandon herself to absence? 'I
think you worry too much,' she said to Gunzel. 'Melek is
devoted to you. The memory of you will warm her in the
cold bed her mother will choose for her.'

Gunzel clutched her handbag as though it were a life-
jacket. 'And what will warm me?' she said intensely. 'I
ask you: what?'

Maddy laughed, abruptly. She was silent a moment
and then laughed again. 'Excuse me,' she said.

Gunzel's mouth trembled. 'Why do you laugh at me?'

'I'm not laughing at you, really,' Maddy said. 'It's just
that I seem to be in the midst of a sea of passion, all
around me little boats are capsizing. Hasan Bey is in an
agony. It is said that Haluk Bey suffers anguish. You are
tormented. I am tormented. Melek is unhappy when you
are unhappy. Only Georgina rides smoothly over the
waves like a flagship of the Cunard line. What kind of
ballast must she be carrying?'

Gunzel was silent for a long moment. Then she said:
'You are tormented?'

'Oh yes,' Maddy said. 'Definitely.'

'Is it the work you are doing that torments you?'
Gunzel said.

Maddy shook her head. 'I don't *like* giving language
lessons at the Institute. That's not what I'd *like* to be
doing with my time. But language lessons could not tor-
ment me. No.'

'Then it's something else . . .' Gunzel said.

'Oh yes,' Maddy said. She watched the swans on the
lake. They were nibbling bits of bread a child had thrown

at them. 'My soul is on fire. That wouldn't be from the lessons.'

'Is there anything I can do to help you, my dear friend?' Gunzel said. 'I would like to be able to help you. Anything . . .'

Maddy turned away from the swans. 'Let's have another drink, shall we? One for the road?'

Georgina sat in the back seat yawning at the landscape. Haluk Bey had been talking volubly for half an hour about the absurdity of American football, as compared with the rigours of Turkish soccer. It was a monologue, requiring no response. Hasan Bey was at the wheel of the car. He smoked one cigarette after another through a squat ivory cigarette-holder. Maddy sat next to him in the front seat. Between puffs Hasan Bey patted her knee. Maddy stared out at the unpopulated countryside. Occasionally she turned her head and looked at Georgina, who smiled back at her wanly.

'How much farther is it?' Georgina said.

Haluk Bey stopped in the middle of a contemptuous sentence and said: 'Aren't you enjoying the splendid drive?'

Georgina sighed. 'The first hour I enjoyed,' she said. 'The second is beginning to pall a little.'

'Don't worry, dear girl,' Hasan Bey said. 'We shall soon arrive.'

'You said that half an hour ago,' Maddy said. 'Half an hour ago we had one more valley to cross, we were in sight of the end.'

'Did I say that, sweetling?' Hasan Bey said.

'You did,' Maddy said. 'Perhaps it's disappeared.'

'What's disappeared?' Georgina said from the back seat.

'Ephesus,' Maddy said. 'Maybe all those tourists have

simply pounded the marble into dust. Or maybe all ruins finally just give up and go away in disgust. What's your opinion?'

'Mine?' Georgina said.

'Yours,' Maddy said.

'I'm beginning to think you may be right,' Georgina said. She lit another cigarette. Haluk Bey had relinquished his soliloquy on soccer and was studying the landscape.

'I think you took the wrong turning,' he said to Hasan Bey.

'Impossible,' Hasan Bey replied.

'Back there at the crossroads,' Haluk Bey said. 'I think you went the wrong way.'

'Oh God,' Georgina said.

'Don't worry, sweetling.' Hasan Bey patted Maddy's knee. 'Everything is all right. We are going on the right road.'

Haluk Bey lowered his head on to the back of the seat and closed his eyes. 'I don't think so,' he said.

'Jesus . . .' Georgina said. 'Are we going to get there or not?'

'*Insallah*,' Haluk Bey said.

'Hasan,' Maddy said.

'Yes, sweetling?'

'I think we should give the matter serious thought.'

'Serious thought?' he said.

'Stop the car,' Maddy said.

'Pardon?'

'I said: stop the car. Now,' Maddy said.

Hasan Bey stopped the car. They all sat vibrating with discontinued motion for a few moments. Maddy felt very tired. She wondered whether she would be able to produce anything other than a dry rattling in the throat now that everyone was silent and waiting.

'I think we should make up our minds whether we're

on the right road,' Maddy said. 'If we're on the wrong road, we should do something to correct that.'

Georgina sighed again and hurled a cigarette butt out the window. 'I'm hungry,' she said.

'I too could eat,' Hasan Bey said, looking over the empty fields on all sides.

'Where is the nearest place to eat?' Maddy said. 'We had no breakfast.'

Haluk Bey laughed. 'American women, always thinking about their stomachs,' he said.

'One should keep one's organs constantly in mind,' Maddy said. 'Their nourishment, growth, maintenance and satisfaction.'

'But why?' Haluk Bey said. 'They will look after themselves.'

'Really?' Maddy said. 'And when was the last time you saw your stomach offering your stomach a stuffed grapeleaf?'

Haluk Bey looked at Maddy with a faint glint of condescension and then lowered his head on to the back of the seat again. 'You Americans always have a smart answer,' he said, closing his eyes. 'Someday you will all give up your smart answers.'

Maddy opened the car door and got out. She massaged her lumbar area and leaned against the fender looking around. A shepherd was watching them from a nearby field. His flock was four. He looked as though he'd been hit a stunning blow between the eyes which had left his face fixed at maximum astonishment.

'Maybe we're his first people,' Maddy said.

Hasan Bey got out of the car. 'What did you say, sweetling?'

'I said, why don't you go and ask that man over there if this is the road to Ephesus?'

Hasan Bey squinted across at the shepherd. 'I couldn't

do that,' he said after a moment.

'Why not?' Maddy said.

'He is a shepherd,' Hasan Bey said.

'Yes,' Maddy said. 'So he is. Is that significant?'

'Significant?' Hasan Bey turned to her questioningly.

'Is there some reason why shepherds cannot be questioned about roads?'

Hasan Bey frowned. 'I would have to go over the field.'

'Maybe he would meet you halfway. Maybe he's a compromising shepherd.'

Hasan Bey studied the shepherd with absorption and then looked at Maddy again and then through the windshield at Georgina and Haluk Bey. Finally he threw down his cigarette with resolution. 'I shall ask that man,' he said. 'Excuse me, my sweetling.' He set off for the field.

Maddy heard Haluk Bey's laughter behind her. He stuck his head out the window and grinned at her maliciously. 'You have made Hasan act beneath his station,' he said. 'A man of Hasan's class does not hobnob with peasants.'

Maddy watched Hasan Bey picking his way through the field. 'Maybe if he only breathes through his nose,' she said. 'Maybe if he washes at the first well we come to . . .'

The village they reached after three-quarters of an hour (going back to the crossroads and taking the alternative turning) had a visible population of three: an old woman wrapped in black from head to foot, with a face the colour of clay, was stacked near the road. When the car passed, her eyes opened for a moment and then closed again; a small grimy boy making copious water against a wall; and an old man with a white beard who sat in a doorway worrying his prayer beads and now and then scratching the hair in front of his ears. The well stood on the out-skirts of the village in a puddle of mud.

'I'm sure that water's not safe to drink,' Georgina said.

Haluk Bey smiled contemptuously down his eagle beak. 'You think it is insufficiently hygienic?' he said. 'Should we have brought our sterilizer?'

'Typhoid is not my idea of a holiday,' Georgina said.

Haluk Bey got out of the car and walked over to the well. There was an old man rooted by the well like a stiff tree. Two black eyes stared out blankly through the white stubble of his face, like two crows nesting in a cornfield. His mouth closed no more without an act of will. He leaned at a considerable angle against the stick which prevented him toppling into the puddle of mud near his feet. Maddy could feel the downward pressure of the body against the frail stick, she could feel the stick resist-ing. Perhaps after they had passed through the village and sometime later, while they were crossing the next valley, the stick would surrender. Maddy closed her eyes and heard the flat suck as the body sank face down into the mud. Or would the old man balance there by the well forever, like a totem?

Haluk Bey exchanged a few words with the old peasant and then stood looking at the well with his hands in his pockets. After a moment he came back to the car and got in. 'Ho-hum,' he said. 'Ho-ho-hum.'

'What do you mean, ho-hum?' Georgina said. 'Is there anything to eat in his place?'

Haluk Bey closed his eyes and lowered his head against the seat again. 'No,' he said.

'No!' Georgina screeched. 'You're kidding!'

Haluk Bey kept his eyes closed. His voice was lazy and insouciant. 'There is water to drink, at this well you see. But there is no café and no restaurant. Women are not allowed in the coffeehouse. In any case, they serve no food there.' He smiled softly with his eyes shut.

Georgina turned her stricken face to Maddy.

'Listen, Hasan,' Maddy said. 'There must be somebody in this village who will sell us some fruit. There's fruit all over this area. An apple would do. A melon. Anything.'

Hasan Bey's eyelids had drooped so low that only whitish slits remained, like slices of almond in a dark cake. He was silent for a moment, the slits aimed at Maddy. Then he turned and looked back down the village road. He said something to Haluk Bey in Turkish. Haluk Bey murmured something in reply and then laughed, without opening his eyes. 'I shall go and ask,' Hasan Bey said to Maddy. 'I shall find something for my sweetling's nourishment.'

'Don't forget your sweetling's dearest friend,' Georgina said from the back seat.

'Indeed no, indeed no,' Hasan Bey said, climbing out of the car. He strode down the road and disappeared through a door. Maddy looked at Haluk Bey. He had put his dark glasses on and she couldn't tell if his eyes were open or if he was sleeping, his head back and a slight smile on his lips. She listened for a moment to his breathing but that gave her no clue. Georgina's face was statuary. She no longer even bothered to smoke. Maddy smiled at her. 'Do not despair,' she said. 'Hasan Bey will provide. I feel it. Something about his eyes.'

Georgina smiled at her limply and looked at Haluk Bey.

'Is he asleep?' Maddy said.

Georgina shrugged. 'Who knows?'

'I am wide awake,' Haluk Bey said. 'I am always wide awake.'

'Oh really?' Georgina said. She lit a cigarette and coughed. 'That's pretty superhuman, isn't it? Listen, Haluk, why the hell don't you trot down the road with your friend and help him carry back the produce? You're not very gentlemanly, are you?'

It was so quiet in the car that Maddy could hear a donkey braying in the next valley. It must be the next valley, she thought. There was nothing in this village that could sustain a donkey.

'Hasan is a very capable person,' Haluk Bey said. 'Very very capable. He requires no assistance. And in any case, I must rest and restore my strength. I do not know what demands will be made on it in the near future.'

Georgina stared at him over her cigarette. Maddy leaned back against the door. Her tongue felt like a long thick rubber slab from her oesophagus to her lips. She sucked it, hoping to provoke moisture.

'Leave him in peace,' she said to Georgina. 'His silence is restful.'

'Your insults do not interest me,' Haluk Bey murmured. 'Occasionally I am saddened by an insult of Georgina but never by yours. There are some women with whom one cannot form a relationship.'

'Only some?' Maddy said. 'Only one such woman now and then?' she said. 'Ninety-nine per cent of your relationships with women are entirely satisfactory, are they?'

Georgina laughed abruptly and slumped down in the seat. 'For god's sake, who cares?' she said.

'Entirely satisfactory,' Haluk Bey said. 'Ninety-nine per cent. Entirely.' He lifted his head from the back of the seat. 'Only now and then there is a woman who . . .' He shrugged and smiled. 'One cannot expect perfection in this life.'

'I see,' Maddy said. She lit a cigarette. The fire burned her throat and made her eyes water. 'Now with Georgina, let me understand this, with Georgina you have one of these entirely satisfactory relationships, a perfect rapport . . .'

'Just stop this crap,' Georgina said. 'It's too hot for this kind of crap.'

'I think,' Haluk Bey said, pulling himself upright in the seat, 'I think it is entirely satisfactory. In its early stages, yes. In the later stages I shall of course expect more.'

'Oh really . . .?' Georgina said. She spat on a handkerchief and rubbed the back of her neck with it. 'I'm going to pass out if I don't have something to eat soon. And some water. We should have had lunch in Izmir. My whole chest has turned to cotton.'

'Of course,' Haluk Bey said. 'But naturally I shall expect more.' He looked at Georgina and smiled lazily. 'Friendship with a woman does not interest me in the slightest.'

Georgina stopped rubbing her neck with the damp handkerchief. Then she turned to Maddy and laughed, just a small piece of a laugh at first, but it ascended like a helium balloon, heading for the open skies.

'Georgina!' Maddy said. 'Stop that at once! The biological burden is enough. I cannot cope with hysteria.'

Georgina stopped laughing and leaned back against the seat exhausted. 'Everytime I relax I have this vision of oranges floating in ice,' she said.

'You ladies are not in a good physical condition,' Haluk Bey said. 'Otherwise the absence of food and water would not affect you so badly. Turkish village women could go for several days without sustenance, if necessary.'

Maddy saw Hasan Bey emerge from a distant door. He was carrying something wrapped in a cloth. It looked to Maddy like the beige head of a baby. He cradled this object in his arms and walked towards the car. Maddy watched his approach with intense concentration. She had to concentrate because of the fierce buzzing in her

44

ears. I am going to pass out, from hunger and desiccation. This is the way it feels. I shall lie down at the side of the road, turning brown, then black, then ash. I shall blow away in the wind. What an end to make. Georgina will be raped as she sits there thinking of oranges in ice. Hasan Bey will hire a photographer to snap the pile of my ash for his album. He will drive sixty miles with his flashbulb at the ready. He will . . .

Hasan Bey opened the door and thrust his bundle inside. Maddy looked at it for a moment. She touched it gently. It was slightly cool. It emanated an odour she could not identify. Hasan Bey crawled in, beaming at her. He seemed several shades darker since she had last seen him. Were her eyes shuttering? Was this the first decline?

'Open it!' he said. 'Open it, sweetling!'

Inside the cloth there was a large slab of goat's cheese, wrapped in a damp gauze. Pieces of the cheese clung to the gauze as Maddy extracted it. Crumbles of the cheese fell moistly on to the seat next to her leg. She held it between her fingers and looked at it attentively. Georgina was hanging on to the front seat, breathing heavily and staring at the goat's cheese. Maddy dropped it carefully back into its gauze.

'Hasan . . .' she said very quietly. 'Hasan, I am not surprised that NATO did not see fit to retain you.'

'Pardon?' he said.

'Kindly go over to that well,' Maddy said, 'and draw up some water for us and while you are there wet your handkerchief so that we may moisten our brows.'

'The well . . .?' Hasan Bey said.

'Do that now, Hasan. Otherwise I shall not be responsible for the mayhem which will follow.'

'I do not understand that word, sweetling. What is this . . . *mayhem*?'

'Violence resulting in injury, Hasan. That's what mayhem is. Don't ask for any further definition. Just go and fetch the water and the wet handkerchief. Otherwise I shall set upon you like a raging beast. You understand raging beast?'

'I think that my sweetling is very angry with me, to my sorrow. But she speaks so quietly! That is unusual in anger. I find that very wonderful.'

'Do you?'

'I do. I find that –'

'Hasan . . .?'

'Yes, sweetling?'

'If you do not bring the water at this very moment I shall beat you about your head until you are senseless. Is that clear?'

Hasan Bey looked at her for a moment and then opened the door and got out of the car. He straightened himself and walked towards the well. The old man rooted next to it lifted his crusty face.

Georgina's hands still clutched the front seat, she clung there like a bird on a rock. Her mouth was very near Maddy's ear. 'I don't believe it, I just don't believe it,' she whispered hoarsely. 'No,' she reaffirmed. 'I don't believe it.'

Haluk Bey laughed. 'You are going to drink the water from the well?' he said.

'Yes,' Maddy said. She stared fixedly at Hasan Bey in the distance. She listened to Georgina's crackling breath near her ear. Later she would murder Hasan Bey: after he brought the water, after they had drunk their fill, she would murder him – stuff his mouth with dry earth and topple him into a ditch, perhaps they would not find him for a decade. And after that, it would be Haluk Bey's turn. Something special for Haluk Bey, something so awful she had not been able to think of it yet. She would have to wait until the water cleared her head. Nothing moved in her brain now but a small hot wind.

'Prepare yourself, Haluk Bey,' she croaked, her eyes fixed on the well.

'I beg your pardon?' Haluk Bey said, lifting his head a little.

'What's taking him so long?' Georgina crackled. 'Is it dry? Is the well dry?'

'No, the well isn't dry,' Maddy said. 'I promise you, the well isn't dry, Georgina.' Was the well dry? Did this village live on the mere hope of water? How could she promise the well wasn't dry? Was she farther along the road to madness than she had perceived? Was this the way the world ended – here in the biblical wilderness with two lunatic Turks? Was this somehow fitting? There was no answer in her head but the soughing of the small hot wind.

Hasan Bey returned to the car with a gourd of water. He passed it through the window to Maddy. In a flush of self-denial she handed it to Georgina. 'Drink slowly,' she said.

Georgina drank very quickly and then gagged. 'I swallowed something,' she said.

'Let us hope so,' Haluk Bey said.

'God knows what it was,' Georgina said. The thought of the hundred things it might be made her heave drily. 'Maybe I'm going to be sick,' she said. 'Maybe I should go somewhere.'

'Give me the gourd,' Maddy said. 'And for god's sake think about something else. Think about Schweppes. Think about gin and tonic with a twist of lime.'

Georgina looked out the window and struggled to place her image. Maddy peered into the gourd. There was a dollop of weed and sediment lying on the bottom, under the slightly greenish water remaining. It came to

47

her clearly what kind of end she would make for Haluk Bey. She would string him head down in the well with his great eagle beak projecting into the muddy weeds at the bottom. Georgina would help her. Perhaps even the Old Totem next to the well would help her, if he sensed her need. Could he still sense anything?

'Take this away.' She passed the gourd to Hasan Bey. 'Then get into the car and drive us to a place where we can get food. We don't care where that is. Anywhere. But it must be nearby and there must be food guaranteed when we arrive. Somewhere here people are eating. It is inevitable.'

Hasan Bey leaned against the side of the car and looked through the back window at Haluk Bey. He moistened his lips with his tongue. He looked across the fields, down the village road, at the Old Totem by the well. He gazed thoughtfully into the gourd. '*Insallah*,' he finally said. 'God willing it so.'

'Marvellous, just marvellous . . . ummm . . . ummm . . .' Ecstatically Georgina pitched meat köfte after meat köfte into her mouth. Her lips shone with olive oil. A group of tomato pips had settled on her left cheek. She swallowed, washed everything down with a carafe of water and then resumed eating. Maddy watched her blankly, listlessly chewing a meatball.

'You are not eating with pleasure, sweetling,' Hasan Bey said, patting her knee. 'Something is wrong?'

She looked at him. In Izmir that morning he had started out burly, almost fluffy, with well-being. As the day progressed he shrank, becoming almost invisible after they drove away from the village with the well. Now he was fluffy again, ripe as a peacock with the attainment of the hillside tavern and the food it miraculously produced. He preened as though the performance were magic. He waited for compliment and gratitude.

'I'm not hungry any more,' Maddy said. 'It's too late to reach my stomach, it has retreated. I catch a faint glimpse of it if I lean out far enough.'

Hasan Bey's disappointment made him look momentarily sallow. Or maybe it was just the sudden effects of the raki he was drinking. It would have been hard to say in the half-light.

'I gather we are not going to make Ephesus today,' Maddy said. 'It would appear the sun is setting.'

Hasan Bey looked over the valley appraisingly. 'Indeed,' he said. 'That would seem to be so.'

Haluk Bey sat at the end of the wooden table perched on the hillside, looking out over the valley with an enigmatic smile. He poured cup after cup of raki from the bottle at his elbow. Maddy had not seen food pass his lips. Food in any quantity seemed to be passing only Georgina's lips. Nothing had ever been known to interfere with her appetite. It revived in an instant, no matter what catastrophe preceded it.

'I am too sensitive,' Maddy said. 'By half.'

'Pardon?' Hasan Bey said solicitously.

'It was of no importance,' Maddy said. 'I have come to soliloquy at last. It was always only a matter of time.'

Hasan Bey sighed. 'Very often,' he said, 'I do not understand what you say, sweetling. I am very disappointed when that happens.'

Maddy lit a cigarette and watched Georgina finishing up the meatballs. She felt vaguely sick. 'It has been a grand day,' she said. 'I shall buy a picture book of Ephesus. Perhaps you can recommend a suitable bookstore, with a wide selection.'

Hasan Bey picked up her hand from the table and pressed it to his lips. '*I* shall buy you a picture book of

Ephesus,' he said gallantly. 'Tomorrow. Early in the morning.'

Haluk Bey laughed without moving his eyes from their contemplation of the valley. 'Hasan,' he said, 'you are a grave disappointment to the lady.'

'I?' Hasan Bey said incredulously.

'You,' Haluk Bey said. He shook his head in a mockery of sadness. 'What a pity, Hasan. What a pity you are such a disappointment to the nice American lady.'

Hasan Bey fumed silently, pouting, blowing air through his squat ivory cigarette-holder.

'That is not quite accurate,' Maddy said. 'In order for there to be disappointment, Haluk Bey, there must first be expectation.'

Haluk Bey turned his eagle beak and studied her blandly for a full minute, swirling the raki quietly around in his mouth. Then he looked at Georgina, who had torn off a piece of bread and was mopping up the olive oil from the empty platter in which the tomatoes had lain. 'You will see something tonight even nicer than Ephesus,' he said. 'I will take you all to my apartment.'

Georgina looked up, her mouth full of oil-soaked bread.

'I doubt we will have the strength to do it justice,' Maddy said. 'Perhaps some other time.'

'Let Georgina answer for herself,' Haluk Bey said. 'She is a big girl and can speak for herself, can you not, Georgina?' He smiled winningly.

Georgina wiped her fingers on a piece of bread and lit a cigarette. 'I feel restored,' she said.

'Oh God,' Maddy said.

'Ready to be amused. I've been very unamused today,' Georgina said.

'Good,' Haluk Bey said. 'Very good.' He looked at Maddy again and bowed mockingly. 'I should be pleased to have you and Hasan as my guests also, if you would like to reconsider.'

Hasan Bey had shrunk again, even his hair looked thinner than usual. He waved his ivory cigarette-holder and said nothing, looking down at the table. Maddy was possessed by a vision of Haluk Bey's eagle beak suspended in the murky well, shot away by a small cannon and a black steaming hole in its place, pierced by a head-hunter's arrow, split into two neat parts by a hatchet. Georgina was examining a torn cuticle.

'I shall hope for a restoration equal to Georgina's by the time we reach Izmir,' Maddy said. 'I shall long for a capacity to be amused by your apartment.'

Hasan Bey was moved and grasped her hand again. 'Sweetling,' he murmured.

Maddy stared into the small circle of the headlights and listened to Georgina giggle in the back seat. Haluk Bey was speaking to her in a low voice that sometimes sounded like a croon. Occasionally he laughed seductively. Georgina made litttle disclaiming sounds and giggled. Now and then a match would be struck and a puff of thin smoke would drift between Maddy's eyes and the circle of the headlights. Hasan Bey concentrated on his driving. The thought of an evening at Haluk Bey's apartment had obviously renewed his spirit. He sat at the wheel discharging excitement. Every few minutes he turned his bright teeth towards Maddy and nodded reassuringly.

'How far are we now?' Maddy said, trying to be heard over the roaring motor and the concatenation from the back seat.

'Not far, not far,' Hasan Bey said. He peered at the mileage indicator. 'Half an hour perhaps,' he said. 'I am driving very well tonight. Half an hour,' he confirmed.

'Half an hour,' Maddy said. She turned her head and

looked out of the window. The black was unrelieved. There were no lights anywhere. 'Why did I bother?' she said softly. 'An artifact is an artifact and will never change its spots like a leopard.'

'What did you say, sweetling?' Hasan Bey yelled.

'I said, in half an hour my last remaining life-force will be spent.'

Hasan Bey looked at her over his shoulder, his mouth slightly open. 'I do not always understand what you say, sweetling. But this will not make a problem for me, I think. I understand you as a woman, yes . . .' He patted her knee, lingered moistly over her thigh. 'As a woman,' he breathed, his long teeth shining.

'Ah yes,' Maddy said. 'That old instinctive communication. I'd almost forgotten about that . . .'

When they returned to the Anadolu Palas there was a message at the desk from Gunzel asking Maddy to come over immediately, on an urgent matter. Once in their room again, Georgina looked at the note, crumpled it up and threw it on the bed in disgust. 'Jesus . . . what a ruse!' she said. 'That girl's like Chantilly lace, she's so transparent.'

'Transparent?' Maddy said.

'Some tragedy, I suppose,' Georgina said. 'Another of Gunzel's tragedies. You'll have to comfort her of course.'

'Who knows?' Maddy said. She went into the bathroom and stared at herself in the mirror. The whites of her eyes were shattered. The eyes themselves protruded. Or had the flesh receded. 'I have aged ten years,' she said.

'We haven't got time for you to go over there,' Georgina shouted from the bedroom. 'Haluk and Hasan are coming for us in an hour.'

'Perhaps twelve years, now that I look more closely,' Maddy said.

'What are you mumbling about in there?' Georgina said.

'Private matters,' Maddy said.

Georgina came and stood in the bathroom door, her hands on her hips. 'I don't know why you can't see what Gunzel is up to. I mean, my god, it sticks out like a sore thumb.'

Maddy leaned over the handbasin and let a little spittle leak down the plug hole. She would have liked to vomit but something in her system was loath to let go. 'What is Gunzel up to, dear girl?' she said. 'Give us the Received Version.'

Georgina glared at her. 'You know perfectly well what she's up to.'

'She has an emergency, by the sound of it,' Maddy said. She pressed a wet towel to her forehead. 'In an hour I shall be fully unconscious.'

'If you'd been sensible and eaten something when you had the chance, you wouldn't feel sick,' Georgina said.

'All of us have not got your incredible resilience.'

'You're changing the subject,' Georgina said.

'What was the subject?' Maddy pressed her temples very hard between her hands and closed her eyes.

'The subject was: are you planning to go over and comfort Gunzel?'

'How do you know Gunzel needs comforting?' Maddy said. 'Maybe she needs money . . . or the address of a male whore . . .'

'Very funny,' Georgina said and slammed back to the bedroom.

Maddy staggered out of the bathroom and lay down on her bed for a moment. Then she lifted herself up and looked at Georgina. 'Tell me,' she said. 'Will you just tell me why it matters to you what the hell I do about Gunzel?'

Georgina picked up her hairbrush and began brushing her hair manically. 'I hate to see you being taken advantage of,' she said finally.

Maddy laughed. 'You're kidding,' she said. 'Even you couldn't say a thing like that seriously.'

'What do you mean?' Georgina said defensively, hair brush in mid-air.

'I mean, dragging me here on false pretences. Waving your bedlinens all the way from Istanbul. Dear Maddy, sweet Maddy, we'll have such a wonderful time in Izmir, everything will be different in Izmir . . .' Maddy rose and returned to the bathroom. She felt that now she might manage to be sick. Something had just come loose in her stomach.

Georgina followed her to the door. 'Listen Maddy . . .'

'Go away and leave me in peace, Georgina. I am going to be so thoroughly sick that I doubt anything will remain of my person. That might temporarily thrill you.'

'Temporarily thrill me!' Georgina shrieked. 'What kind of a fat-ass do you think I am?'

'Unfortunately, I know what kind of fat-ass you are. Now please go into the bedroom and close the door. I don't want to upset you with the violence of my organism.'

Georgina looked uncertain for a moment and then backed away, pulling the door shut as she went. Maddy fell to her knees on the tiled floor next to the toilet and vomited three times, with thirty-second intervals between each seizure. Then she got up, brushed her teeth, gargled, washed her face and returned to the bedroom. Georgina was sitting on her bed studying her hairbrush attentively. She looked up when Maddy came in. Her eyes glistened with tears.

'Oh Christ,' Maddy said.

'I can't help it,' Georgina said. 'It's what you said in there.' She pointed to the bathroom. 'About me bringing you here on false pretences . . .'

'But you did bring me here on false pretences!' Maddy said. 'I knew your pretences were false before we left Istanbul. I forgive you, I always do forgive you. So far. You're a tease, that's all.'

Georgina leapt up furiously. 'I am *not* a tease! Nobody has ever called me a tease.'

'Well, maybe nobody was as unrestrained as I am,' Maddy said. 'Because it couldn't be more apparent.'

Georgina clenched her fists and the vein in the middle of her forehead bloomed. 'As a matter of fact, I didn't promise you *anything*. You just *hoped* it would all work out here, you just *imagined* it might. But I didn't *promise* you anything.'

Maddy shrugged. 'All right,' she said. 'You didn't promise me anything. I dreamt up the whole thing. I'm a fantasist.'

'Ooh!' Georgina said. 'Jeeesus . . . damn . . .' She sat down abruptly on the bed and hammered her knees with her clenched fists.

'You're going to have a haemorrhage if you're not careful,' Maddy said. 'You're a glutton. Gluttons are haemorrhage-prone.'

Georgina stopped hammering her knees and sat very still staring at the floor and breathing heavily. Slowly the breathing subsided into normality. Her head remained averted.

'Have you gone into a catatonic state?' Maddy said. 'Nod three times if you hear me.'

'I remember it all very clearly,' Georgina said. 'I remember the night we first talked about coming here together. I remember very lucidly everything I said.'

Maddy shuffled through the litter on the bureau, looking for a match for the cigarette gripped in her teeth.

'Are you interested or not?' Georgina said.

'I'm not interested in your revision of history,' Maddy said.

'I'm not revising anything,' Georgina said. 'I am reminding you of what happened.'

Maddy found a match, struck it and inhaled luxuriously on her cigarette. 'But dear girl, I *know* what happened. I was there. Remember?' She looked at her watch. 'If you don't hurry, Haluk Bey is going to discover you in your chemise.'

'Damn Haluk Bey!' Georgina said.

'Well! That's a change,' Maddy said. 'I thought Haluk Bey was a comer. I thought I perceived all the signs of that condition.'

Georgina stood up, her eyes as narrow as knives. 'All I ever said to you was that I thought it would be fun for us to go to Izmir for the Cumhuriyet holiday. That's what I said. Period. I never said I was going to come here and have an orgy with you. I never promised I'd . . .'

Maddy puffed her cigarette and looked out of the window that opened on to a covered alleyway. The wall opposite appeared to continue into the heavens. It was grey and splashed irregularly with pigeon droppings. She wandered over and sat down on her bed and folded her arms and studied Georgina carefully, squinting through her cigarette smoke. 'There you lay,' she said, 'clutching your little blouse to your ample bosom, frightened out of your Michigan wits. There you lay,' she smiled fondly, 'just one step from total disaster, refusing to open your eyes. I remember saying to you, over and over: dear girl, do open your eyes and look at me.' She blew out a frayed elliptical smoke-ring. 'These are the memories that warm one's heart in later years,' she said.

Georgina was silent but open-mouthed.

'Your pubic hair was exceptionally delectable that night, I remember,' Maddy said. 'It was like many little soft ringlets, curled up heartbreakingly around your –'

'Will you shut up!' Georgina said, rising from her bed. 'Will you just shut up!'

Maddy shrugged. 'Most women enjoy hearing what delightful creatures they are. I could go on, I could become positively Elizabethan.'

'Just shut up!' Georgina said. 'I don't want to hear what a delightful creature I am. I don't want to delight you. I don't want to hear anything about it.'

'Poor Georgina,' Maddy said. 'Poor dear girl. Life is very difficult, isn't it? Fraught with difficulties.'

Georgina's face struggled into its glacial aspect. Her mouth snapped to like a trap on a rabbit. She turned to the foot of her bed and knelt down by her suitcase. She took out a sheer black blouse and a pair of stockings. She carried these into the bathroom and closed the door. Maddy snuffed out her cigarette, sighed and lay back. She felt very tired and weak and pure since she had been sick. She felt like a broken reed made whole again.

Georgina came out of the bathroom wearing her sheer black blouse. The white skin underneath shone like the gleam from a very distant lighthouse. Her eyebrows lay smoothly near her hairline. The oblique eyes glistened like Fool's Gold in a rock formation. She stopped at the bureau and applied Chanel No. 5 to her earlobes, her thighs, and the soft concavity where her shoulders flowed into her breasts. Maddy watched her calmly from the bed. Then she got up, found a pair of slacks in her suitcase and began climbing into them. Georgina turned around.

'What are you doing?' she said.

'Dressing,' Maddy said.

'In slacks?'

'In slacks. Why not?' Maddy said, tucking her shirt in.

Georgina's eyes narrowed with suspicion. 'Where are you going?' she said.

'To comfort Gunzel.' Maddy sat down to put her socks on.

'You can't do that!' Georgina said. 'Hasan Bey expects to see you tonight.'

'Then he'll be disappointed, won't he?' Maddy said. She stood up and slipped her belt through the loops.

'Maddy!' Georgina screamed.

Maddy stopped slipping her belt through the loops and looked calmly at Georgina.

'I don't want to go without you,' Georgina said. 'You've got to go.'

'Now that's logic for you,' Maddy said. She picked a cardigan off the back of a chair.

Georgina came over to her, arms outstretched beseechingly. 'Maddy, you can't do this to me, damn it . . . what will I say to Hasan when he shows up here?'

'Tell him I've gone over to seduce a friend,' Maddy said.

Georgina collapsed in a heap on the floor. She pounded the carpet with her fists. 'I don't want to spend the evening alone with Haluk. You can't desert me this way.'

'You should have considered that possibility when you made the date with him,' Maddy said. 'Besides, the most that can happen is that he'll fling you into bed when you've drunk enough to inhibit whatever scruples you still have. That's a nice normal activity, perfectly respectable and blessed by society. What's the problem?'

Georgina looked up at her from the floor white-faced.

'The problem is,' Maddy continued, 'that it's no fun with Haluk Bey unless I'm there to see it – old Maddy, aching with frustrated passion. Without your audience, Haluk Bey is just another agitated prick. He might of course be a bit more lethal than your run-of-the-mill, common-or-garden type prick.'

Georgina picked herself slowly up off the floor. She brushed her hair out of her eyes and refastened one of her stockings which had come unhinged from the garter belt. Then she sat down on her bed and lit a cigarette. 'You're not really going to seduce Gunzel, are you?' she said.

'You knows?' Maddy said.

'You couldn't *want* her . . .' Georgina said disconsolately.

'She might be restful.'

'Since when did you want a rest?' Georgina said.

'Since this afternoon,' Maddy said.

'Listen Maddy . . .'

'Don't make any promises you can't keep,' Maddy said. 'One more broken promise from you and I'll bash your head in without compunction.'

Georgina was silent for a moment, smoking. Then she said: 'I'll bet Gunzel isn't restful at all. I'll bet she's awful. Just awful. She's so nervous. And all that clutching. And hysterical. And she'll think if you make love to her once that you've made some kind of lifelong vow and she'll hang around your neck like an albatross until you're seventy-five.'

'Have you finished?' Maddy said.

'No,' Georgina said. 'I haven't finished.'

'Well, finish,' Maddy said.

Georgina got up from the bed and came over to Maddy and put her arms around her neck. Then she kissed her clumsily on the mouth and went on standing in front of Maddy with her arms lying around her shoulders as though they had died there.

'You have such a practical arrangement with your parts,' Maddy said.

'What's that mean?' Georgina said.

'Such an instrumental arrangement. That's the kindest way to put it. Seduce Maddy, you tell them. And up they rise for work.'

Georgina dropped her arms. 'You bitch,' she said.

'Now I, on the other hand,' Maddy said, 'never have to tell my parts anything at all. They're privy to all my secrets and usually get wherever we're going first, before I have a chance to issue a command.' She kissed Georgina's eyes and began unbuttoning her sheer black blouse.

'What are you doing?' Georgina protested.

'I am on the point of making love to you,' Maddy said. 'To anyone else, that would be obvious.'

'We can't make love now!' Georgina said, backing away from Maddy. 'There isn't time.'

'As someone – I forget who – once said: we'll make time. Now take off that garter belt.'

Georgina emitted a little muffled sound which Maddy took to be a scream of sorts and moved back towards her bed.

'Some little girls start things they can't finish,' Maddy said. 'Little girls like that have to learn.'

'Maddy, darling . . . this isn't the place . . .'

'You prefer the street? The street! Like a common wench! Believe me, this is much nicer.' Maddy pushed her against the bed and Georgina sat down heavily. Maddy knelt down and loosened her suspenders and rolled her stockings off. She kissed her ankles. Her calves. She breathed heavily against her thighs.

'Stop!' Georgina screamed.

'Stop? Maddy looked up. 'Whatever for?'

'Just . . . don't go on,' Georgina said. 'I'm . . . not ready. The moment isn't . . .'

'Oh but the moment is, dear girl!' Maddy said. 'The moment couldn't be more.'

'I'm too nervous,' Georgina said. 'Haluk is probably waiting downstairs in the lobby right now.'

'He'll just think you're making yourself especially attractive for him. And he'll be sure of it when you arrive in the lobby beautifully flushed from your bed of love.' Maddy encircled her, slipped off the sheer black blouse and unhooked the lacy bra underneath. Then she rocked back on her heels. 'Lean forward, dear girl,' she said.

'This is absolutely crazy,' Georgina said. She leaned forward and the bra fell into Maddy's lap.

Maddy sat on her heels looking at Georgina's breasts for a moment. 'Now, what do I think of those . . .' She put her hand out and touched the left nipple contemplatively. 'That would require much reflection.'

Georgina smiled nervously.

Maddy shifted forward to her knees. 'Shall we finish this unveiling, dear girl? Shall we do that now?' she said. She leaned against Georgina's bed, breathing in draughts of heated Chanel No. 5 from underneath which there gradually arose the moist fresh scent of the skin's rainforest. 'I am compensated for your character defects,' she said. 'At least I will tell myself that for the moment.'

'Don't insult me, don't insult me,' Georgina murmured, closing her eyes. 'How many times have I asked you to stop insulting me.'

They were an hour late. The Beys were sitting at a small table on the edge of the closed dining-room staring at each other silently across the remaining half of a bottle of raki which had been sent out for in desperation by the desk clerk. Hasan Bey got up when he saw Maddy step out of the elevator. Haluk continued leaning against his fist. He fingered his glass and gazed into the dark interior of the dining room.

'Sweetling . . .' Hasan Bey kissed Maddy's hand. He

looked slightly haggard. 'I was beginning to worry that you suffered from your migraine again.'

'No, no, no,' Maddy said. 'A thousand times no. Do you want to kiss Georgina's hand too – in lieu of Haluk Bey's attentions?'

Hasan Bey looked startled. 'Georgina's hand . . .? He recovered himself. 'I would be honoured . . .' He picked up Georgina's uninterested hand. 'I see that neither of you has suffered from our adventure today. I am very happy to see that.'

'Absolutely no pain,' Georgina said.

'Is your friend joining us?' Maddy said.

'My friend . . .?' Hasan Bey looked anxiously towards Haluk Bey, who still sat head on fist at the dark little table on the perimeter of the dining-room. 'Haluk Bey is feeling a little . . . tired.'

'A little tired?' Maddy said. 'What a pity. Perhaps we should call off our date.'

'Oh no!' Hasan Bey said. 'Please do not do that.'

'Jesus . . .' Georgina breathed. 'If it's going to be like that . . .'

Haluk Bey rose, emptied his glass and turned in a single arc of movement. He stood very tall and straight, like a torero before the bull. He gazed upon Maddy and Georgina with an expression of sorrowful malice. His black eyes were luminescent, the nostrils of the eagle-beak subtly dilated, the thin lips curled upwards almost imperceptibly. The cheekbones on which the globes of his eyes rested were a pale ledge.

'Why, he's beautiful!' Maddy exclaimed. 'Anger suits him.'

Haluk Bey walked slowly towards the trio transfixed by the elevator. He seemed to emanate a faint shimmering glow. Like foxfire from a swamp, Maddy thought. 'So you have decided to join us after all . . .' he said. 'We have so looked forward to your presence.' He looked from Maddy to Georgina and back to Maddy again. His enormous black eyes narrowed slightly. 'You are both looking extremely . . . fetching,' he said.

Georgina giggled nervously. Maddy looked steadily into Haluk Bey's glittering eyes. 'We are both extremely well,' she said. 'I can't think when I've felt better. Recently.'

Haluk Bey nodded, lowering his eyes. 'Good,' he said. 'Very good. I like to hear that. Women are so often . . . indisposed, isn't that so? They are so changeable, are they not?'

'Are they?' Maddy said.

'Fickle Woman, as the saying goes,' Haluk Bey said.

'Does it?' Maddy said.

'Come on, let's go,' Georgina said. 'Let's get out of this dark hole.' She walked towards the door. Haluk Bey stood looking at Maddy for a moment. The thin lips parted slightly in a smile, revealing a row of small misaligned teeth. 'Ah yes . . .' he said. He turned and followed Georgina out. Hasan Bey stood limply at Maddy's left hand. At Haluk Bey's exit the circles under his eyes deepened.

'You don't seem very happy tonight, Hasan,' Maddy said.

'Do I not?' Hasan Bey said. He laboured mightily and managed a weak smile. 'Oh, but I am very happy, sweetling. Your wonderful person always makes me very happy.'

'Grand,' Maddy said. 'I'm delighted to hear it.' She took his arm and steered him towards the door. Georgina and Haluk Bey were already sitting like two stiff dolls in the front seat of Haluk's Mercedes. Both stared silently out of the tinted windows. Maddy crawled into the back seat. Hasan Bey lurched forward slightly as Haluk Bey pulled away from the kerb. He regained his balance. He sat next to Maddy stroking his tie compulsively. Georgina chain-smoked.

'You are being very quiet tonight,' Haluk Bey said to Georgina.

'I just feel quiet,' Georgina said, lighting another cigarette.

'I miss that hard edge to your personality,' Haluk Bey said, negotiating a curve. 'You are soft tonight.'

'Soft, soft,' Maddy said from the back seat. 'I could use a drink.'

'You will have a drink at my place,' Haluk Bey said. 'I have everything to drink. Do you know why it is that Georgina is so very soft tonight?'

'Georgina is a big girl and can answer her own questions,' Maddy said. 'Where is this place of yours?'

'Overlooking the bay,' Haluk Bey said. 'The splendid Bay of Izmir.'

'That's nice,' Maddy said. She patted Hasan Bey's limp hand. 'Hasan loves a good view.'

Maddy drank her whisky and studied the small glass jar that contained it: there was a Peter Pan Peanut Butter label affixed to one side. At the bottom of the label was printed: not for sale in the U.S.A. Maddy picked at the label with her index finger and looked out the large scenic window at the Bay of Izmir.

Hasan Bey appeared at her elbow, drinking brandy out of a tall American jelly glass. 'It is a very wonderful apartment, is it not?' he said to her confidently. 'There is nothing like it in Izmir.'

'I don't find that hard to believe,' Maddy said. She finished her whisky and held out the Peter Pan Peanut Butter jar to Hasan Bey. 'About the same as last time,' she said.

64

'Haluk Bey has only the finest quality whisky here. Only the very best,' Hasan Bey said proudly, accepting the empty jar. 'I am very happy that you drink it with delight.'

'Sheer delight,' Maddy said.

She lit a cigarette. Hasan Bey disappeared into the kitchen with her peanut butter jar. She spent his absence studying the northwest to southeast crack across the scenic window. There was a fascinating section just in the middle of its course where the glass had shattered into a small ice-field. It must have been, she thought, the point of impact.

When Hasan Bey returned with her whisky, he looked ruefully at the crack in the glass and said: 'Haluk Bey can be very virile when he is drunk.'

'Virile?' Maddy said.

Hasan Bey shrugged. 'I suppose he will replace the glass some day.'

'Virile?' Maddy repeated.

'When he is drunk,' Hasan Bey said.

Maddy scratched at the label on the peanut butter jar and looked around the crack in the window for a while, wondering what Haluk Bey and Georgina were doing upstairs. They had disappeared an hour before, Georgina carefully carrying with her a gin and tonic in a plastic coffee-mug. For the first fifteen minutes Maddy had heard their footsteps overhead but since then there had been only an unrelieved silence.

'What's on the other side?' she said.

'The other side?' Hasan Bey said.

'Of the Bay,' she said. 'Over there . . .' she pointed.

'That is called Karsiyaka – the Other Side,' he said solemnly.

'I see,' Maddy said.

'Perhaps you would care to drive there tomorrow?' Hasan Bey said.

'Perhaps,' Maddy said.

'There is a small café there on a hillside. We could drink cognac,' he said.

'We'll talk about it later,' Maddy said.

'There is a very marvellous view of the city from the café.'

Maddy nodded. There were still no sounds from upstairs. Had Haluk Bey entered his condition of drunken virility? Caused a northwest to southeast fissure in Georgina's face and fled already into the night in his silver-grey Mercedes? She considered for a moment how she would react to a defaced Georgina. And then she wondered whether she should be ashamed of that and decided she wouldn't be.

'What's upstairs?' Maddy said. She took a large gulp of whisky. It made her eyes water.

'Nothing,' Hasan Bey said.

'Nothing?'

'Very little,' he said. 'It is not much used, the upstairs.'

'Except on such occasions as these . . .' Maddy said.

'I beg your pardon, sweetling?'

'Perhaps we should have a look,' Maddy said. 'I'd like to see the full extent of this very wonderful apartment.'

'Oh no,' Hasan Bey said, alarmed. 'We must not go up.'

'Why not?'

'Haluk Bey would be angry.'

'Would he?' Maddy said.

'Oh yes.'

'Why would Haluk Bey be angry if his guests joined him, Hasan? That seems very inhospitable of him.'

'He will invite us upstairs when he is ready,' Hasan Bey said. 'Now I must go and get myself another brandy. It is very marvellous brandy.'

He vanished into the kitchen again. Maddy heard him unstopper a bottle. She walked over to the circular tile staircase that worked its way up from the ground-floor garage to the mysterious rooms of the top storey. She listened, sipping her whisky. Then she turned and walked across the room to a Louis Quatorze chair and sat down. Hasan Bey was obviously having two marvellous interim brandies before he appeared again with his filled jelly glass. She looked to the right and straight into the ruby eye of a huge alabaster bird. It resembled a hybrid of the North American eagle and the South African vulture: there was something expectant coupled with the grandeur. And its neck was too thin. Maddy got up and looked at the bright red eye: was it a real ruby? Someone had gouged a channel around the eye with a crude tool and there were assorted scrapes and chips in the folded wings. A section of the vulture-ruff was missing. It was two and a half feet high and stood on a rickety wooden base. She heard Hasan Bey swishing his brandy behind her.

'That is a genuine ruby,' he said. 'It is very valuable.'

'Really,' Maddy said. Cracks of red had appeared in Hasan Bey's eyes: it was as though they had been shot during their period in the kitchen and were hopelessly bleeding to death. 'Where does Haluk Bey get all his money?' Maddy said.

'From his father,' Hasan Bey said.

'And what does his father do?'

'He imports. He is an importer. A very important man. He is most of the time in Europe. He is not very much in Izmir.'

'And Haluk Bey takes care of the business here . . .' Maddy said.

Hasan Bey looked discomfited. 'Haluk Bey . . .' He stopped. He began again, more confidently. 'Business is not Haluk Bey's *métier* . . . you know that word, *métier*? It is French.'

'Oh?' Maddy said.

'Not his *métier*,' Hasan Bey repeated. His eyes had reddened another degree. 'Nor mine, nor mine,' he said. 'However,' he shrugged, 'we cannot always choose.'

'What would Haluk Bey rather do?' Maddy said.

Hasan Bey leered at the alabaster bird, at the same time dropping his arm around Maddy's shoulders and giving them a squeeze. 'Can you not guess that, sweetling?' he whispered.

'One cannot buy one's pilaf with that,' Maddy said. 'One cannot repair one's scenic windows.'

Hasan Bey chortled, clutching his jelly glass. 'You have a very wonderful sense of humour, sweetling. Very wonderful.'

'Thank you. Shall we go upstairs now?'

'Not yet, sweetling. Not yet. Are you not happy down here with me? Are you not pleased to be, once again, alone with your Hasan?'

'Thrilled to bits,' Maddy said. 'But I'd rather be alone with you upstairs.'

'But we wouldn't be alone upstairs!' Hasan Bey protested.

'Such is the feeling between us, my dear Hasan, that we could be all alone in the midst of a crowd of people. Is that not so?'

He smiled at her redly, looking a little unfocused. 'Ah . . . that is true, sweetling. That is very true.'

She led him gently towards the circular staircase. Their arrival at the bottom step shocked him into focus again. He recoiled in horror. 'We cannot go up there until Haluk Bey has called for us,' he said. 'That is impossible. If I did such a thing, I would cease to be a friend of Haluk Bey's.'

'That doesn't seem like much of a friendship to me,'

Maddy said. 'If it can't weather a little thing like going upstairs . . .'

'He does not wish to be intruded,' Hasan Bey said. 'He is with a lady.'

'So I believe,' Maddy said. 'I have a dim recollection of arriving with one.'

'And he wishes to be alone with her.' Hasan Bey lost his frantic explanatory tone and dropped both arms around Maddy, pressing his jelly glass into the small of her back. 'As I wish to be alone with you, sweetling,' he breathed thickly into her ear. 'There is a sofa over there, do you see it? We can practise. We must do some practice before you leave the city.'

Maddy remained rooted for a moment. She stared over his shoulder into the ruby eye of the indeterminate alabaster bird. She smelled the aromatic ear which lay against her right cheek. Then she put both hands against his chest and pushed: he spun across the parquet flooring and fell down heavily next to an ornate nineteenth-century French telephone that rested on a wooden box in the corner. Hasan Bey looked stunned but he had managed to keep his jelly glass upright. He took a swallow out of it and crawled to his feet. He brushed the seat of his trousers and looked across at Maddy curiously and then fondly. 'A passionate woman,' he said. 'A very wonderful passionate woman.'

He came towards her with his arms outstretched, the jelly glass carefully vertical. Maddy braced herself against the balustrade of the staircase and prepared for the onslaught. At that moment Haluk Bey descended the stairs and stood very still on the last step looking at Hasan Bey and Maddy.

'There is a great deal of noise coming from down here,' Haluk Bey said. 'It is interfering with my concentration.'

'Is it,' Maddy said. 'Are you playing statues?'

'I do not understand your reference,' Haluk Bey said. 'However, the point is, I do not like rowdiness. Hasan, my friend, can't you be more discreet?'

'I beg your pardon, Haluk Bey. I am very sorry for the noise. I am very regretful if we have disturbed you.'

Haluk Bey inclined his head seigneurially towards Hasan Bey, closing his eyes for an instant. Then he looked at Maddy for a moment before turning to go upstairs again.

'Just a minute, Haluk Bey,' she said. Behind her she could feel Hasan Bey's shudder. 'I feel obliged to mention that I have never spent so boring an evening in the last fifteen years. Nor have I ever seen so ungracious a host in any other house.'

There was a full minute of silence while Haluk Bey contemplated the top of the stairs, one hand on the stair-rail. 'I am sorry to hear that,' he said without turning. 'Fortunately, such judgments do not bother me. Perhaps it is your own fault that you are so bored. Hasan Bey is usually considered charming company by other ladies he has known. Perhaps there is something lacking in your response to him.'

'Yes, yes . . . I agree!' Maddy said. 'I fully agree. The element lacking in my response is interest. You've put your finger right on the source of the trouble. Clever old Haluk Bey . . .'

Haluk Bey turned and looked down the stairs at Maddy. For a moment she thought he was going to lose control, rush down the steps and envelop her in what would prove a fatal embrace. But the struggle was short-lived. He smiled tightly from under his eagle-beak, he drummed a brief message with one hand on the stair-rail. 'It is too bad,' he said, 'that you have not the powers of appreciation shown by your friend Georgina. I have not heard her complain this evening of boredom or an

70

ungracious host. On the contrary . . .'

'Georgina,' Maddy said, 'has an extremely erratic sense of boredom: it comes and goes like the wind. Perhaps by the time you get upstairs again you will find that she has fallen into a coma of ennui. She can do that in the twinkling of an eye. Perhaps you didn't know that.'

'I do not require you to tell me about Georgina,' Haluk Bey said. 'I know about Georgina. Perhaps it is you who do not know Georgina.'

Maddy laughed, wildly she thought: surely this was what could be described as 'wild laughter.' She noticed that it floated through the room just as wild laughter was reputed to do in all the women's magazines she had ever come across in doctors' waiting-rooms. '*Not* know Georgina!' she said. '*Not* know little Georgina! God, how lovely it would be not to know little Georgina, how really delightful to cancel out all knowledge of her, not a trace remaining, the way it was with botany . . .'

'Botany . . .?' Hasan Bey interposed. 'I do not under–'

'Quiet, you,' Maddy said. 'Refill your jelly glass and open your mouth from now on only to drink the first-quality brandy.'

'You must not insult Hasan Bey,' Haluk Bey said. 'He is a friend of mine.'

'There's a friend of *mine* sequestered upstairs,' Maddy said. 'Kindly tell her we're leaving.'

Haluk Bey ran one hand slowly over his very black glossy hair and smiled, showing all his small crooked teeth. 'I am not holding your friend prisoner,' he said. 'If she wishes to leave, she is free to do so. Would you like to ask her yourself?'

Maddy had a quick vision of herself running pell-mell up the steps (sweeping Haluk Bey casually over the stair-rail en route), shoving a drink-sodden Georgina towards and down the stairway, into a taxi, and back to the sweet confines of the Anadolu Palas. But she realized she would never make it: she would be seized on the way up either by Haluk Bey, who would welcome the chance to break her neck in the ensuing struggle, or by the trusty hench-man whose brandy supply depended on it. And in her ears she could hear Georgina protesting her removal, could see Georgina petulantly sinking even deeper into lubricious cushions, closing her eyes, refusing, while Haluk Bey's misbegotten teeth gleamed luminously from the dark stair-well. It would not be a good scene.

'For God's sake, what's all the conversation about down there!' Georgina's voice drifted lazily down from somewhere above. Maddy looked up and saw her stand-ing at the top of the stairs, one hand on a hip thrust forward. She was in her stocking-feet. Her hair was down. Her other hand, arched from the wrist, held a cigarette. She looked like an illustration from *Criminal Romances*: 'Pictured is Miss Georgina Frabish, the "other woman" in the infamous triangle which completed its tragic course last Tuesday night . . .'

Maddy took a deep breath and sprinted up the stairs, slithering by an astonished Haluk Bey like a playing card under a door. She stopped just in front of Georgina, pant-ing a little.

'Jesus . . .' Georgina said. She took an involuntary step backwards.

'Put your shoes on and come with me,' Maddy said. 'Now.'

'What . . .?' Georgina said.

'You will be eaten like jelly beans at a Scouts' Jamboree.'

'What *are* you talking about?' Georgina said. 'It's early yet.'

'It's later than you think. Will you put your shoes on?'

Georgina looked down at her stocking-feet and wriggled

her toes pleasurably. 'Why should I put my shoes on? I like my feet this way.'

'You're drunk,' Maddy said. 'You look like a Forty-Second Street whore and you're drunk into the bargain. What must I have been thinking of!' She leaned very near Georgina's face. 'That man with the small messed-about teeth, midway down the stairs, has it in mind to introduce you to an Izmirean debauch. I don't think it's going to be quite what you had in mind from years of reading the *Ladies Home Companion*.'

'A debauch!' Georgina exclaimed. 'Haluk Bey is far too depressed to be interested in that sort of thing. He wouldn't have the strength. All you ever think about is sex. It's disgusting.'

'Maybe you *should* be eaten like jelly beans,' Maddy said. 'Maybe that's your fate and I shouldn't interfere with fate. Why must I be so headstrong?'

'You're the one who's drunk,' Georgina said.

'You see,' Haluk Bey said softly from behind Maddy's left shoulder, 'she is not a prisoner.' He circled Maddy and reached Georgina. 'She is enjoying herself. She has a great capacity for enjoyment.' He touched Georgina's arm and smiled at her tenderly. 'She is a woman of great sympathy, also.' He faced Maddy. 'Unlike yourself,' he said, closing his eyes briefly from the pain of it.

From the corner of her left eye Maddy glimpsed the beginnings of a deep depression in the parquet floor. She moved her head and followed the two white gashes from the top of the stairs across the floor to the large windows on the far side. It was as though a man with razor legs had for some years been dredging a canal. There was a banquette ten inches off the floor and covered with soft rugs against one wall. Maddy observed Georgina's shoes, at right angles to each other, leaning against the side of this couch. Against the wall opposite was a pile of suitcases and boxes. A rope was strung across the middle of the room, one end tied to a window handle and the other to a short length of pipe projecting from the wall. The purpose of the pipe was not immediately apparent. Thrown across this piece of rope was a maroon shirt and a pair of coffee-coloured socks. The room was otherwise empty, except for Georgina's plastic coffee-mug and another peanut butter jar belonging to Haluk Bey, which stood side by side on the floor next to the couch.

'Charming room,' Maddy said. 'Stark. I like that. No useless clutter of objects.'

Haluk Bey smiled bravely and looked down at Georgina. 'She does not like our room,' he said. 'It is perhaps too simple for the elaborate American taste.'

'Oh I *like* the simplicity. I do, yes . . .' Maddy said. 'No pandering to sybaritic tastes for sitting down or leaning or anything like that. I'm devoted to leaning myself, especially on festive occasions. But I admire people who can take it or leave it alone.'

'She loves her comfort,' Haluk Bey said sadly to Georgina. 'Comfort before all. No regard for the spirit of things. Even for love. How very Western . . .'

'The Ringling Brothers might buy this act,' Maddy said. 'But you'll have to get Hasan Bey a clown-suit.'

'Now look . . .' Georgina said. 'Can't I just have a drink or two in peace, without a scene or anything? Can't a girl just have a quiet drink? I mean, what's wrong with you, anyway?'

'Wrong with me?' Maddy said. 'Why, nothing's wrong with me, Georgina Frabish. Nothing at all. I've been downstairs with Hasan Bey for nearly two hours, drinking whisky out of a peanut butter jar and trying to stay awake so I can enjoy this tremendous cracked view of the Bay of Izmir. At the risk of upsetting Haluk Bey's aesthetic sense, I must mention that I am extremely hungry and it is now past eleven o'clock. If ever I thought before that I'd been really genuinely threatened by psychic annihilation, I take it all back. Not till tonight did I realize how clandestinely it could come upon one. And upstairs – nestled sweetly in her furry rugs, ears ringing with gin – is my friend Georgina, who plays games. Who thinks the bogey-man will always go away if she just tells him they don't do things like that in Michigan.'

Georgina looked stunned. She picked tobacco off the end of her tongue and stared at Maddy. Haluk Bey smiled into the room as though he did not choose, out of politeness, to notice that someone in his presence had gone mad.

Georgina's eyebrows finally descended a little. 'You never open your mouth except to insult me,' she said. 'Besides, you exaggerate everything. All I'm doing is having a quiet drink and listening to Haluk Bey's problems. Aren't we supposed to be interested in other people's problems? Are we just supposed to be selfish egotistical monsters, for God's sake?'

Maddy sighed, turned, and began walking down the stairs.

'Where are you going?' Georgina yelled.

'To the Anadolu Palas, if I can get by that nit downstairs. Although by now he's probably drowned in his jelly glass. There must be some reason for that lovely silence.'

'You're going without me?' Georgina said.

'Yes. Without you,' Maddy said, descending. 'All alone. Restfully, beautifully alone.' She paused midway on the stairs. 'On second thought, I think I'll call on a friend. I hesitate to mention this, in case you'll think I'm using it to promote your leave-taking. But I'm not. I'm simply announcing an idea that just occurred to me. You have a good time.'

'But . . .' Georgina said.

'I'll leave a small light burning by your bed,' Maddy said.

She found Hasan Bey in the kitchen, leaning against the counter and staring fixedly at an empty brandy bottle. 'Well, Hasan . . . now there's a sad scene. I'm sure if you rummage around, you can find something else to drink. Perhaps some very wonderful cleaning fluid. Goodnight.'

'Goodnight?' Hasan Bey opened his mouth very wide in an attempt to focus his eyes, which had died by now from loss of blood.

'Goodnight,' Maddy repeated. She turned and walked out of the kitchen and down the tile staircase. She squeezed around the fat Mercedes in the thin garage and hailed a taxi in front of the apartment house. She felt too tired to cope with Gunzel and her urgent matter. It was almost midnight, her hunger pangs had progressed into nausea, and she was a little drunk. On the other hand, she felt too vulnerable to face the pea-green interior of the room at the Anadolu Palas. She gave the driver Gunzel's address. She settled back on the split vinyl seat-covers and closed her eyes. She listened to Georgina perform her seductive laugh; she watched Georgina lift her eyebrows to the level she had discovered, through years of experimentation, to be the most aphrodisiacal; she heard the tinkling Chinese-garden-chimes voice – quite unlike the voice in which Georgina commanded tea from waiters, inquired about hotel rooms, or reported that the bathwater was hot. Maddy's head became a mad cacophony of Georgina-sounds, an insane collage of Georgina-sights. She opened her eyes in self-defence. She groaned slightly – the reason why, she could not tell. But the driver heard nothing over the roar of his pre-war motor.

'You seem not to be listening to me,' Gunzel said. 'Perhaps I am mistaken but you seem not to be listening . . .'

Maddy stared into her brandy, wondering if she should lie down. 'I am hearing other voices, other rooms,' she said.

'You are not well tonight,' Gunzel said, with finality.

'That's true,' Maddy said. 'But I must not over-complicate. Maybe it's just the brandy.'

'You are drinking so much tonight because of Georgina,' Gunzel said. 'I don't know why you permit her.'

'Why I permit her . . .' Maddy said. 'That is a long and hair-raising story. Meanwhile, there is your own problem. I am listening to it with at least one-quarter of my consciousness. That's all that's left over. Maybe it will be enough.'

Gunzel's lips trembled. She held a handkerchief to her mouth and shook her head slowly back and forth. 'Dear God,' she sobbed.

'I really find all this hard to understand,' Maddy said. 'Of course in my present state I would find the Pledge to the Flag baffling.'

Gunzel removed the handkerchief from in front of her mouth. 'Why is it hard to understand?' she said. 'I have explained it to you with care.'

Maddy lowered her head into her hands. She pressed the brandy glass against her right temple. 'The sky is falling, said Henny-Penny. I just found a piece of it in my chicken feed.'

Gunzel leaned over and grasped the cognac decanter and held it towards Maddy.

'Why are you trying to keep me in this lamentable condition?' Maddy said. She held her glass out and Gunzel tipped the decanter into it.

Gunzel settled into the divan cushions with her soggy handkerchief and pouted at Maddy. 'I don't understand you tonight,' she said.

'You don't.'

'Your mind seems to wander and you speak in riddles. You only care about Georgina. You don't care about me in the least.'

'That's an exaggeration,' Maddy said. 'I am most perturbed by your problem. I cannot think what one does with a pregnant maiden who can't understand how she got that way. It is extremely ungratifying to be devoted to a female who believes it possible to be impregnated by virile pussy-willow pods.'

'Melek does not believe it was a pussy-willow pod that was responsible,' Gunzel said. 'Why do you say these things?'

Maddy smiled, feeling the corners of her mouth reach all the way up to her ears. She waited for her mouth to resume its normal horizontal but it remained where it was.

Gunzel stared at Maddy's mouth. 'Perhaps all this seems very silly to you.'

'No, no. Not silly. A trifle absurd. But not in the least silly.'

Gunzel wiped her eyes. 'Dear God, I don't know what to do . . .'

'I suggest you accept Melek's condition with grace. Perhaps there will be an eventual shrine in her village.'

'You are making sport with me,' Gunzel said.

Maddy smiled her hyperbolic smile.

'I thought you were my good friend . . . I need your help,' Gunzel said wetly.

'Since I do not perform abortions, I can only offer you my sympathy.'

'Abortions! My God . . .' Gunzel slumped against the cushions. 'She would never have such a thing . . .'

Maddy closed her eyes and considered Georgina's face for a moment. It was very large and lurid, like a poster at the Penny Arcade. 'I cannot understand why you should care that Melek is With Child,' she said to Gunzel. 'You have been fed up with her for years. You said only the other day that she is unsatisfactory. And now it would seem that she also has a lover. Why don't you just let Melek take her foetus back to the village in peace?'

Gunzel let out a moan of pain and got up from her divan. She paced rapidly between the divan and the glass door to the balcony, kneading her handkerchief. 'She shouldn't have done this to me . . . she had no right to treat me this way. And when I said to her: Melek, what have you done! she said to me – I swear it – she said: I don't know, it is all a mistake.'

Maddy swirled her brandy and closely examined the chased copper top of the table in front of her knees.

'How could it be a mistake? I said to her . . . if you slept with a man you must have noticed it!'

'One would think so,' Maddy said, swallowing brandy. 'However, Melek is intensely absent most of the time. Perhaps her downfall occurred during one of the periods when she was away from her head.'

Gunzel stopped pacing and looked fixedly at the wall behind Maddy's head as though she were watching with disbelief a movie starring the newly-ripe Melek. She shook her head. She lifted her heavy handkerchief to her lips. 'I do not understand how she could have done such a thing to me,' she said. 'Her mother will take her away to the village and lock her up.'

'Ah . . .' Maddy said, one elbow resting on the chased copper table, 'if more mothers locked up more maidens, would catastrophes be averted, or merely private?'

Gunzel sat down heavily on the divan. 'You are simply amused by all this. You do not see that she has humiliated me. You do not see that it is a disaster for your friend Gunzel. Everyone will laugh at me. I will be alone.' She clipped herself hard on the side of the head. 'Dear God, why did she do it? How could she be so stupid!'

'You should have told her about things,' Maddy said. 'You should have informed her what happens in this life when semen travels through all those little tunnels and dark rooms and finds some egg with its head turned.'

'I never thought . . .'

'Ah well . . .' Maddy said. 'It's hard to imagine a brain so inviolate.'

'She does not know how to turn her head without instruction,' Gunzel said. 'She is not so *clever* as a sheep in the field.'

They sat across from each other in silence for a moment: Maddy tilted over her brandy, Gunzel sunk into her cushions.

'I don't suppose she knows who the father is,' Maddy said, 'since she considers the whole thing a case of air-borne seed.'

'She cannot remember *anything*,' Gunzel said shortly. 'Completely nothing.'

'Not even an afternoon that seemed a little more plea-surable than most, but she couldn't quite put her finger on it?'

'Nothing,' Gunzel said, fixed in her cushions as though irremediable. 'Oh boys, yes. She remembers boys. This boy, that boy – the ones that are always here and there. There was tea one day, coffee another day, this time a film, that time the Hachette Bookshop, then there was a swim at the beach. All as usual. Boys she has known for years, since childhood. Here and there she sees them. But she remembers nothing. She goes through life in a dream. I must say to her, Melek, eat now. Melek, it is time for bed. You must not cross the road now, Melek, or else you will be passed over by a motor-car. All she knows how to do is knit. She knits everywhere, day and night.'

'Apparently, she has dropped a stitch at least once,' Maddy said.

Gunzel glared at her, then tears began rolling from her large eyes again.

'Please stop crying, Gunzel,' Maddy said. 'You will erode yourself.'

'I know you are bored by me,' Gunzel said. 'I am sorry to be such a boring friend.'

Maddy lifted her elbow off the chased copper, leaned back in her chair and closed her eyes. All the disparate sips of brandy gathered themselves into a wave and pulled the roots of her eyes into her stomach. Down there she discovered it was after all Georgina's mouth and she couldn't get out of it.

'I think I must lie down, Gunzel,' she said. 'It may already be too late to discuss it.'

She felt Gunzel's hand on her arm and looked up into Gunzel's wildly kinetic eyes. 'Surely your face hasn't always looked like Las Vegas?' she said. She got to her feet and with Gunzel's hand still exerting a firm pressure on her arm, she wobbled into an adjacent room and fell on to another divan. It was like descending suddenly into a nest of Persian kittens. She smelled a soothing musk aroma just before the spinning stopped, along with everything else.

She woke up with the sun warming her feet through a broken slat in the closed shutters and the rest of her body in cool shadow. She lay swathed in soft rugs amid a ring of brocade pillows. She did not move for several sybaritic moments. Her spine ran like water along the contours of the divan. Her head was as cool as sherbet. Her breath moved in and out lightly, with no catch in its rhythm. Her body had not yet realized that her brain was awake. It was the blissful moment before union.

Then she turned her head slightly to the right on its brocade pillow and her eyeballs began to pulsate wildly. A very white ringing commenced in her ears. Through the ringing she heard a murmur of voices in the next room. They were too inharmonious to be angelic. The door opened and someone tiptoed across to the divan. Maddy struggled to focus her broken eyes in the half-light.

'I have brought you coffee,' Melek whispered. 'Would you like to drink it now?'

'I would, yes, I would like to drink it now,' Maddy said. She sat up very slowly and took the tray from Melek. 'What time is it?'

Melek was silent a moment, trying to read her watch through the shadow. 'It is half past eleven,' she finally said.

'My God,' Maddy said. 'Where's Georgina?'

'Georgina?' Melek said.

'She was with me last night.'

Melek hesitated. 'Gunzel said nothing of Georgina.'

Maddy sipped her coffee and considered. 'She didn't come here with me,' she said at last. She put down the cup, handed the tray to Melek and dropped her feet over the side of the divan. 'Where are my shoes?' she said.

Melek bent over from the waist, holding the tray very carefully, and peered along the floor.

'It would help if we opened the shutters,' Maddy said.

'Yes . . .' Melek said. She opened the shutters.

Brilliant light streamed into the room. Maddy squinted into it like a mole and waited for Melek to retrieve her shoes, which had been dropped under a chair by the door. Maddy leaned forward very cautiously and put them on. She stood up. The ringing in her ears increased. She could see her heartbeat in each eye. 'Have you an aspirin?' she said to Melek. 'Perhaps several aspirin?'

Melek smiled at her tremulously for a moment and disappeared with the tray. In two minutes Gunzel appeared with a bottle of aspirin and a glass of water. Her eyes were very red and her face was swollen. 'Did you sleep well?' she said to Maddy, almost reproachfully.

Maddy swallowed three aspirin and nodded. 'I think so,' she said. 'But it seems I have misplaced Georgina.'

Gunzel shook her head. 'You left her at Haluk Bey's. So you said to me last night.'

'At Haluk Bey's?'

Gunzel shrugged. 'That's what you said last night. But you had been drinking very much. Perhaps you left her somewhere else.' She sat down on the end of the divan and stroked one of the rugs as though it were a puppy. 'Georgina is not a good influence. She makes you unhappy.'

'Yes, she does,' Maddy said. 'But it doesn't seem an important consideration.'

'You are a very strange person,' Gunzel said. 'Everyone wishes to be happy.'

'Where is my dress?' Maddy said. 'I know I had a dress with me.'

Gunzel rose and extracted the dress from the tall German-style wardrobe against the far wall of the room. She handed it to Maddy.

'I thank you for attending to my needs last night, Gunzel,' Maddy said. 'I regret that I was too drunk to advise you on your newest problem, which is strangely burned into my memory this morning, although I cannot remember where I left Georgina.' She stepped into her dress. 'I suppose your mother is now quite certain that all infidels are debauched as well as damned.'

'She is not in the house,' Gunzel said. 'She is with her sister in Bursa. In any case, you helped me very much last night. I could not have endured it to be alone at such a time.'

Maddy ran her hands through her hair. 'I must have brought a comb. I never go anywhere without a comb.'

Gunzel pointed to the head of the divan, where a handbag stood propped against a leg. Maddy picked up the handbag. 'I'll go and freshen up a bit,' she said to Gunzel. 'I wish I could rinse my brain out . . . it feels as if lots of small dirty people have been camping in it.' She disappeared into the hallway.

When she came out of the bathroom she heard Gunzel's voice in the kitchen and went in. Melek was sitting downcast at a table in the corner. Gunzel stood at the stove making fresh coffee. They both fell silent when Maddy entered. Melek blushed.

'Am I interrupting?' Maddy said.

'Not at all,' Gunzel said, watching the long-handled ladle in which her coffee bubbled away.

Melek looked up at Maddy and then lowered her head again quickly.

'I was just saying goodbye to Melek,' Gunzel said without turning. 'She is going away tomorrow.'

Melek pressed her cheek with one hand and stared at the marble floor.

'Is she?' Maddy said. 'Must she?'

Gunzel took the coffee ladle off the burner and set it on the counter. 'Yes, she must,' she said. She took two small cups down from a rack.

'I see,' Maddy said. Her eyes were beginning to recover a little. They no longer pulsated as frequently but they felt extraordinarily covert, since they seemed to look out from between large mounds of swollen flesh. Maddy rather liked the impression that they couldn't be seen.

Melek began to weep quietly. Gunzel looked at her angrily and handed Maddy her coffee.

'It doesn't seem that Melek is very happy about going,' Maddy said.

'I am very unhappy,' Melek sobbed. 'Gunzel is very angry with me.' She pulled distractedly at her long blonde hair. She leant over the small table and wept.

Gunzel sipped her coffee. 'I am angry, yes, I am angry,' she said. 'Why shouldn't I be angry? Such a stupid girl. So now you will go home. To your mother.'

Melek continued to weep over the table. 'What will I do without you?' she said to Gunzel.

'Look what you have done *with* me!' Gunzel screeched. 'There is no hope for you.'

Melek stood up, trembling the length of her tall unassertive body. She wiped her eyes with the palms of her hands and stared disbelievingly at Gunzel, who gazed fixedly at the tiled wall above the stove. Then she ran from the room. Gunzel leant against the kitchen counter to steady herself.

'Perhaps we should sit down somewhere to drink our coffee,' Maddy said. 'You look a bit palish.'

Gunzel took her cup over to the small table Melek had just vacated. She sat down. Maddy joined her. 'I must go soon,' Maddy said. 'I have to locate Georgina.'

'Georgina . . . Georgina . . . that's all you ever think about,' Gunzel said. 'What about me? What about Melek?'

'I thought things had been settled,' Maddy said. 'She's going home to her mother. To be locked up.'

'Don't make jokes,' Gunzel said. 'It is a tragedy.'

'I'm not making jokes. Isn't she going home?' Maddy said.

'Dear God, what else can she do!' Gunzel slumped in her chair with a groan, one hand to her forehead.

'Now Gunzel,' Maddy said. 'Take hold of yourself. Things will work out. She isn't the first fallen maiden, you know.'

'In this country,' Gunzel said, 'it is a serious matter. A

very serious matter. It is no laughing-matter.'

'In no country is it a laughing-matter,' Maddy said. 'It's just that some women in every country laugh anyway.'

'I am not one of those,' Gunzel said, pulling herself upright again. 'Melek is not one of those either.'

The slits through which Maddy's eyes looked had widened a little more. Air was circulating in her rods and cones. It was a good feeling. 'You consort all the time with Western women,' she said. 'You begin to *feel* like Western women. You do all the things Western women habitually do, including the evil things. And then you get pregnant and suddenly you're Turkish again and it's the end of the world.'

Gunzel studied the thick sediment in the bottom of her coffee-cup for a moment. Then she said: 'To be a woman of this country, it drives you crazy.'

'Why doesn't she marry someone,' Maddy said, 'instead of making a forced march back to the village?'

'Who would marry her?' Gunzel said mournfully.

'One of those boys you told me about last night. One of those here, there and everywhere boys she's known since childhood.'

'They wouldn't marry her,' Gunzel said. 'They are children. They only want to play. If Melek wanted one of them to marry her, he would be suspicious.'

'Why?' Maddy said.

'Because they know that Melek is not interested in marriage. She is only interested in knitting,' Gunzel said.

'I find that hard to believe in the circumstances,' Maddy said.

'I assure you,' Gunzel said, 'she never thinks in her head, deeply, of anything else. She is not like us.'

'Oh,' Maddy said.

'And if one of those boys found out that she is

pregnant . . .' Gunzel said, 'they would all try to sleep with her but no one would marry her. Ever. They are pigs.' Gunzel let the judgment hang blackly in the kitchen air. She spread her palms on the table and sighed. 'It is not New York City,' she said.

'So you will spirit her off to the village,' Maddy said, 'where she will produce the infant in the privacy of the family olive grove and then she will come back to Istanbul – willowly as ever, leaving the little cousin behind with a wet nurse.'

Gunzel gazed at her with intense melancholy. 'She will never come back to Istanbul. She will stay behind the shutters in her mother's house until a husband has been found for her and then she will go to his house and that will be the end of her.' She was silent a moment, then she shuddered. 'A peasant,' she said, 'who wears muddy boots up to his knees and has a space between his front teeth.'

Maddy prodded the grounds in her cup. They looked as black and rich as humus; perhaps something grew in there? Then she stood up. 'I will ring you up tonight and see what's been decided,' she said to Gunzel. 'I have to go now, I really do. I'm distracted. Georgina may have been done away with, for all I know.'

Gunzel nodded sadly, tears glistening in her eyes. 'It has already all been decided,' she said. 'Melek must accept her fate.'

Maddy looked down at the top of Gunzel's head and was silent for a moment. 'Why not marry her off to a man?' she said finally. 'Not to a boy she's known since childhood. To a man. Preferably one she hardly knows at all. Just like in New York City.'

Gunzel considered this. 'What man?' she said.

'Haluk Bey is better than Hasan Bey, since he's richer and better-looking. But Hasan Bey would be easier.'

'Hasan Atabeg?' Gunzel said incredulously. 'You mean Hasan Atabeg?'

'The very same,' Maddy said. The solution had come to her with the sudden blinding force of absolute rightness. 'He's ideal.'

'Ideal!' Gunzel exclaimed.

'He would cherish the wedding photograph forever. It would be the apex of the album – very large, maybe twenty inches by thirty inches, on glossy paper. He would probably travel around with it on tours. Melek could stay at home and knit.'

Gunzel looked at her speechlessly, making strange little backing-away movements, although she was still sitting down. 'You are joking again,' she said quietly, so as not to disturb Maddy's equilibrium.

'It is no joke,' Maddy said, with rich certitude. 'It is the alternative to the shuttered house and the muddy boots.'

Behind Gunzel's eyes Maddy could see calculations begin. Her mouth dropped open with concentration. 'She would live here, in Izmir,' she said.

'Presumably,' Maddy said. 'I don't think Hasan Bey will be offered a job at the U.N.'

'Or perhaps they could move to Istanbul,' Gunzel said.

'With a little encouragement Hasan Bey could be moved anywhere. As long as he is permitted to take his very modern furnishings along.'

Gunzel leaned back in her chair, her eyes glazed with premeditation. 'Ah . . .' she said after a moment. Then her face darkened. 'But she does not know Hasan Bey. There is no time,' she said despairingly.

'She will know Hasan Bey by tomorrow night,' Maddy said. 'I will personally arrange an introduction. He is mad about blondes. Four-fifths of all the ladies in his album are blondes. Melek has a natural advantage.'

'Why,' Gunzel said intently, 'would he wish to marry Melek?'

Maddy thought for a moment. 'He would not wish to marry anyone,' she said. 'The wish will be inspired in him. The wish will be provoked. Melek is a rich blonde girl who has travelled in France, yes. Her mother owns olive groves — many olive goves. The best brandy is served at her table. She eats Circassian chicken every night. She loves to dance the rhumba. She never blinks when the flashbulb goes off.'

'What are you saying?' Gunzel said anxiously.

'I am saying the programme,' Maddy said. 'Melek hardly speaks at all, which is helpful. She must practise her French.'

'I do not understand,' Gunzel said helplessly. 'I think you are making a joke of this tragedy.'

'No, no!' Maddy said. 'I have always wanted to tamper cynically with a human life. Now here is Melek, whose life must be tampered with at all times or it simply falls on its face. This is a God-given opportunity. I probably won't have another one.'

Gunzel was silent for a moment. 'What if Melek . . . refuses?' she said finally.

'Does Melek want to return to a village of thirty-five souls? Does Melek want a peasant with muddy boots and gappy teeth? Does Melek want to leave her indispensable friend who tells her when to cross the road?' Maddy walked triumphantly to the kitchen door. She turned. 'I cannot speak in Melek's place. I cannot propose to her on Hasan Bey's behalf. Some things they will have to manage for themselves. With your help, because I have no time left over from my own emotional horrors. Don't ask me to draw the curtains and pull back the bed covers and bake the wedding cake. All right?'

Gunzel sighed. 'I sometimes think I do not understand Western women at all, even though I have spent so many years among them,' she said. 'It seems to me that you are not being serious.'

'I am so serious,' Maddy said, 'that my head is spinning from it. I am intensely earnest about marrying off Melek to Hasan Bey – I think they are meant for each other. I think they will be happy together – Hasan with his fifteen-foot German phonograph and Melek with her knitting and you. It's true that some marriages are made in heaven. I never realized it until now.' She pushed open the kitchen door and smiled reassuringly at Gunzel. 'Now I really must go and attend to my agonies. I will ring you in the morning and tell you what to do.'

'Yes . . .' Gunzel stood up, tentative.

Maddy turned halfway through the door, waiting.

'I really intended to say to you . . .' Gunzel began. She stopped. She looked a little confused. Maddy continued through the door, a mad smile on her face all the way down to the street.

She went back to the Anadolu Palas and found the pea-green room empty. The beds had not been slept in and the chambermaid had carefully piled Georgina's discarded clothing from the night before on top of a suitcase. Maddy went downstairs again to the desk clerk and made inquiries. The clerk smiled at her knowingly from under his tiny moustache and said that Miss Frabish, like herself, had not returned to the hotel since the previous night and that there was no message.

Maddy went back upstairs and fell exhausted across her bed. Her head ached from her eyes all the way down her spine and driblets of saliva kept rising into her mouth and then retreating, so that she expected to vomit at any moment but was unsure if she was strong enough to get up for it. It will be, she thought, the first time I have ever fouled my own nest. She wept unrestrainedly for ten minutes and then in intermittent spasms for another twenty and then instead of going downstairs to eat lunch – which she knew to be a sensible step to take – she fell asleep. When she woke up again it was four o'clock in the afternoon. She lay on the bed feeling flat, empty and white. She did not know if she could rise from the bed. She did not know whether she wished to.

Then the door opened and Georgina came in.

'Well . . .' she said. 'What happened to you?'

Maddy gazed at her imperturbably and was silent.

Georgina threw down her little sequined evening bag and began unbuttoning her sheer black blouse. She hummed 'That Old Black Magic' softly under her breath. 'You'll never guess what,' she said, kicking her shoes off. She waited. Maddy was silent, eyes fixed upon the ceiling. 'What's wrong with you?' Georgina said accusingly. 'Are you sick?'

Maddy pulled herself up on one elbow and groped for a cigarette on the night table. Georgina stood holding her black blouse in one hand and watching her. Then she draped the blouse over a chair and unzipped her skirt. 'Do you want to guess what?' she said.

'No,' Maddy said. 'I do not want to guess what.' She inhaled on the cigarette and felt the veins in her eyes dilate.

'I'm engaged,' Georgina said gaily. 'Can you believe it?'

Maddy tried to close her eyelids over the gargantuan veins but was unsuccessful. She stared at Georgina and let her cigarette burn in the ashtray. 'What did you say?' she said.

'I said, I'm engaged. To Haluk Bey. Isn't that amazing?'

'You are engaged to Haluk Bey,' Maddy said.

Georgina flung her skirt over the chair. 'We decided last night. I mean, really, it was early this morning. To be accurate.' She pulled on her bathrobe. 'How was Gunzel?' she said, tying the sash.

Maddy snuffed out the cigarette and sat up on the side of the bed. She massaged her temples for a moment, then she lit another cigarette. 'You are,' she said very calmly, 'the emptiest thing since a menopause tit.'

Georgina dropped the fringed ends of her bathrobe sash and looked at Maddy with her mouth open and her eyes wide.

'You have not,' Maddy continued, equally calmly, 'anything inside your head but cold cream and snippets from Vogue magazine and tiny selected bits of *Dover Beach*.'

'Now listen,' Georgina started.

'If I live to be 105 and meditate on it every day until then I will never understand how I could ever have been the Adoring Fool of such as you. Surely it could not be just your neck and shoulders. Perhaps I was smitten by your implausibility. I suspect I'm being too easy on myself.'

Georgina pulled at her bathrobe sash until she was cinched in like an antebellum lady. 'I'm not going to stand here and be insulted by you any more. That's finished.'

'Yes,' Maddy said.

'I mean, you're sadistic. You just *thrive* on putting me down. *You* never loved me. And now you insult me because I'm engaged to this wonderful guy. You just can't understand how anybody would want a normal life with a wonderful guy.'

Maddy puffed her cigarette and watched the purple and red spots in the corners of her eyes. 'Haluk Bey is of course a wonderfully normal wonderful guy,' she said. 'Just like blueberry pie. You might even survive the first year. Be sure and send your mother your full address and register with the American Embassy.'

Georgina snorted. 'Haluk said you'd be like this.'

'Did he?' Maddy said.

'Oh, he's not stupid, you know. He said you'd try to talk me out of it, since you hate him so. He said you'd say every ugly thing in the book to me.'

'I wouldn't dream of trying to talk you out of it,' Maddy said. 'I think he deserves you. I think you deserve each other. I am surrounded by romances, real and potential – all made in heaven. It's a bumper year for predestination.' Maddy got up and walked towards the bathroom. 'Excuse me,' she said. 'I'm going to take a bath.'

Georgina came to the bathroom door after a minute and watched Maddy leaning over the tub testing the water. 'You don't really need me,' she said to Maddy. 'You've got Gunzel just waiting for you, licking her chops. And God knows how many other women just around the corner.'

Maddy straightened up, listening to the blood run down from her head. 'That's quite right, I don't need you. I never have *needed* you. What would I need you for? I just *wanted* you at one stage. Now I don't want you anymore. It's a good feeling.'

Georgina considered for a moment. 'You don't just stop *wanting* people all of a sudden.'

'Oh yes you do,' Maddy said. She stepped into the tub. 'All of a sudden. It's like a miracle.' She settled back in the hot water up to her chin and closed her eyes. 'I wish you a felicitous engagement,' she said. 'Now go away and close the door.'

Georgina sat down on the side of the tub and looked at

Maddy. 'You couldn't have stopped wanting me since last night,' she said.

Maddy opened her eyes. 'What are you trying to do, collect everybody? Aren't you happy with just old Haluk Bey?'

'I mean, people don't just change overnight.'

'Oh that happens, that happens,' Maddy said. 'Given the proper *coup de grace*. Now run along and close the door.' She narrowed her eyes and watched the steam rising from the water.

Georgina brooded, dipping her dressing-gown sash in the bath water. 'I expect Haluk Bey and I will have a wonderful life together.'

'I expect so,' Maddy said.

'He's really a brilliant person. Full of ideas.'

'I'm sure,' Maddy said.

'He's had very sad experiences with women. It's made him sort of melancholy, you know. But he says I can pull him out of that.'

'Pulling people out of things is really your forte,' Maddy said.

'I really had no idea I'd fall for him like this,' Georgina said, wringing out her sash-ends.

'I certainly believe that,' Maddy said.

'I'm not doing this out of revenge, you know.'

'Revenge?' Maddy opened her eyes wide.

'I'm not just doing it because of you and Gunzel.' She rubbed a brown crack in the porcelain.

'Me and Gunzel . . .?' Maddy said.

'I mean, sure I was angry last night when you ran out on me and went off to see her. But I wouldn't get *engaged* to somebody because of a thing like that.'

Maddy swallowed some hot water and laughed. It was a thin watery laugh that went nowhere. 'Of course you wouldn't, she said. 'What a quaint idea.'

Georgina stood up and studied her face in the mirror over the handbasin. 'Was she as nice as you thought?' she said casually.

'Did I think she'd be nice?' Maddy said.

'Oh I think you thought she'd be sort of nice,' Georgina said, making little spitcurls on her forehead. 'Was she?'

Maddy smiled and swallowed a little more of the hot water just under her chin. Georgina waited a moment and then shrugged. 'Well, it's your business. I was just anxious for you to find someone nice. You deserve someone nice.'

'You're such an awful hypocrite,' Maddy said. 'In addition to all your other awfulnesses.'

'I am *not*,' Georgina said indignantly. 'I really mean that. I want you to have the best.'

'Ho ho,' Maddy said.

'Just because I've decided to marry somebody, that doesn't mean I've stopped caring about you.'

Maddy sat up in the tub and squinted at Georgina across the steam. 'When will the wedding be?' she said.

'Oh, I don't know exactly. Sometime in the spring, I think.'

'And you'll go back to the Institute until then?' Maddy said.

'Oh yes,' Georgina said. 'I'll keep my job. I need to buy some things, you know. A kind of trousseau . . .'

'And Haluk Bey will come to Istanbul every couple of weeks to see you, will he?'

'Sure,' Georgina said. 'Couldn't keep him away.'

'And when Haluk Bey's not in town, you'll be skipping into my room for little conversations and things, I expect . . .'

'Well, if you'll *let* me.' Georgina smiled winningly.

'And then after you marry Haluk Bey in the spring,

you'll live here in Izmir, is that right?'

Georgina took the combs out of her hair and let it drop across her shoulders. She shook her mane. 'I guess we'll live here. Haluk's work is here.'

'But you'll come to Istanbul often for visits and to shop and that sort of thing . . .'

'I couldn't stay away from Istanbul very long. You know how crazy I am about the place.'

'Yes I do,' Maddy said. 'So you'll visit often. And when you visit, you'll come around to see me, won't you? We'll have dinner together, something like that?'

'Well, I'd *love* that,' Georgina smiled fondly. 'That would be terrific.'

Maddy leaned across the tub, both hands gripping the porcelain sides. 'Wouldn't it? Wouldn't it just be terrific,' she said. 'Well, you can forget it, you seamy bitch! I have one absolutely unbreakable rule – devised at this very moment but it couldn't be more unbreakable if I'd had it since childhood – I never, no, absolutely *never* mess about with engaged ladies. I don't chat to them or eat with them or offer them the refuge of my bed. Engaged ladies are off-limits. Engaged ladies are, as it were, invisible.' She sat very still looking at Georgina, who stared back at her, eyebrows at maximum elevation. Maddy thought she noticed through the steam that Georgina's mouth was twitching in one corner. 'If I were you,' Maddy said very quietly, 'with the future you have in store, I'd encourage Haluk Bey to make it a Christmas wedding. Because otherwise you might just die off in the interim from lack of entertainment. Your blood might just turn to powder. You can't tell.'

The twitch in the corner of Georgina's mouth was more conspicuous.

'Now,' Maddy said, 'will you take yourself out of here and leave me in peace? And close the door when you go.'

Georgina moved slowly to the door and then turned and looked at Maddy, who had dropped back into the water and was observing the tops of her toes rising from the water at the other end of the tub. 'You're a cruel woman,' Georgina said. 'A cruel, cruel woman.'

Maddy wriggled her toes. 'Cruel women do not just grow like cabbages,' she said. 'Old French saying.'

Georgina went out. Maddy heard her shuffling around in the bedroom for a while, then there was silence. Maddy got out of the tub and into her bathrobe. She towelled her hair and brushed her teeth. She inspected her eyes in the mirror. The whites were beginning to look slightly more creamy but the lids were puffy and pinkish. Pinkish eyelids, Maddy thought. Christ.

She went into the bedroom and found Georgina asleep in her slip and panties. She was lying on her stomach, stretched full out, with her arms flung over her head. Maddy looked at her a moment and then began to dress.

After she had finished eating supper in the dining room downstairs and had drunk three very strong, sugarless coffees and a brandy afterwards, she rang up Hasan Bey.

'Listen, Hasan,' she said. 'I'm ready to take you up on your invitation to visit the Other Side. Tomorrow would be lovely for that.'

'Tomorrow?' he said. 'The Other Side?'

'I know you had a long and turbulent evening, Hasan, but try to collect yourself. You wanted to take me to the Other Side, to a hillside café with a view of the city, remember? Well, I feel just in the mood for that tomorrow afternoon. It strikes me as a perfect thing to do. All right? When will you pick me up?'

'Uh . . .' Hasan Bey struggled to collect himself. He coughed and was silent for a moment. Then he said: 'I must see when I can arrange a car. I thought you did not want to see me again.'

'People often get that idea about me. I don't know why. It must be my very wonderful face,' she said.

Hasan Bey was silent again on the other end of the line. 'Yes,' he finally said, uncertainly. 'You have a very wonderful face.'

'Fine,' Maddy said. 'Now, what time will you be here?'

'Have you heard about Haluk Bey and your friend Georgina?'

'I've heard.'

'Is that not good news?'

'Marvellous news,' Maddy said. 'I wish them every happiness.' She thought she heard Hasan Bey laugh a very soft laugh but she couldn't be sure it wasn't just static on the wire.

'I will come for you around two o'clock,' he said. 'It will take us only a short time to drive there. You will like it, I think.'

'Where exactly is this hillside café?' she said. 'So I can orient myself.'

'Oh it's just off the main road, up a hill there. You can see it from the road. It is a very marvellous place.'

'With a very wonderful view of the city,' Maddy said. 'I'm looking forward to it.'

'You are a very strange woman, I think,' Hasan Bey said. 'Oh a marvellous woman, yes. But very strange.' He paused. 'Last night I thought . . .'

'Don't think about it, Hasan,' she said. 'Just don't think about it. I'll see you at two o'clock.'

'Till then, sweetling . . .'

Maddy put the phone down and then picked it up again and asked for Gunzel's number. 'Gunzel?' she said. 'Are you ready for instructions?'

'Maddy, I don't know . . .'

'You have no nerve, Gunzel. You really must practice

98

having a little nerve. It's very attractive in people.'

'I'm just worried, Maddy ... I never know what Melek will do. Maybe she will ruin everything ...'

'Maybe she will,' Maddy said. 'But you must remember that Hasan Bey hardly notices anything but colour of hair and eyes. Even if Melek does something unfortunate we may still have a chance. But you've got to develop some nerve.'

Gunzel was silent a moment.

'Are you still there?' Maddy said.

'Yes,' Gunzel said. 'I'm here. What are the instructions?'

'That's the spirit!' Maddy said and lit a cigarette.

When she got back to the room Georgina was sitting on the side of the bed brushing her hair. Her eyes were still glazed with sleep and seemed to sit in her head even more obliquely than usual. She looked up for a moment when Maddy came in and then continued brushing, her eyes fixed on some interior point.

Maddy squatted down by her suitcase and after some rummaging around drew out a notebook with a ballpoint pen clipped to the front cover. She sat down on her bed, dragged the suitcase on to her lap, put the notebook on top of it, and began writing.

Georgina pulled a long hair out of her brush and held it up against the light as though she were inspecting it for mites. 'What are you writing?' she said.

Maddy did not look up.

Georgina shrugged and brushed again for a few minutes. Then she said: 'Come on ... what are you writing in that notebook?'

'Why do you care?' Maddy said, not looking up.

'I'm just curious,' Georgina said, brushing again. 'That's all.'

'Really.'

Georgina went into the bathroom and ran the water for a moment. She came out again wiping her face with a towel. 'I can't seem to wake up properly,' she said. 'Part of me is still asleep.'

Maddy looked up, ballpoint poised. 'Part of you is always asleep,' she said.

Georgina threw the towel angrily onto the bed and glared at Maddy. 'I've never known anybody like you,' she said. 'You can't be nice to anybody for a minute. You think you're so goddamned smart.'

Maddy flipped two pages back in the notebook, read for a moment, and then scratched out a word.

'Are you writing something about me?' Georgina said.

'Of course,' Maddy said.

'Don't you *dare*!' Georgina said.

Maddy looked up. 'You're not presuming to interfere with my personal liberties, are you?'

'What are you going to do with that?' Georgina pointed to the notebook.

'I thought I'd run it off on the Institute's mimeograph machine and then disseminate it.'

Georgina stared at her disbelievingly. 'You're joking,' she said.

'Why would I be joking?' Maddy said. 'The world should have the opportunity to know that there's more to life than Dick and Jane and Spot. Don't you think?'

Georgina dropped upon her bed, aghast. 'I never thought for a moment . . .' she gasped.

'You've just gone through life thinking consequences were funny things like Abominable Snowmen and nobody ever really saw one,' Maddy said. 'Now you're going to see one.'

Georgina put her hands over her mouth. Her famous eyebrows had almost disappeared into her hair.

'Now, don't be alarmed,' Maddy said. 'There's no cause for alarm. I won't use your real name of course. I'll refer to you as Madam X.'

Georgina fell back on her bed with a moan. 'You're vindictive,' she said. 'You're trying to ruin me.'

'Ruin you?' Maddy said. 'How could I ruin you? On the contrary, your social life will probably pick up immensely. People will admire you for being so flexible and untainted by prejudice. There'll be queues of this kind and that outside your door. Brava! they will call through your window. Brava, Georgina!'

Georgina sat up again and looked at Maddy, shaking her head slowly from side to side, tears glistening in her eyes. 'I never thought I'd see the day you would do this to me,' she said. 'After what we've been to each other.'

'Careful now, Georgina,' Maddy said. 'You're lapsing into *Woman's Own* again.'

Tears dripped down Georgina's face. 'That you could forget so quickly . . .' she said.

'Forget?' Maddy said. 'Oh, but I haven't forgotten anything. The whole experience is permanently sealed into my head. Now it will be permanently sealed into yours. I'm a little concerned at the way experience leaks out of your head almost as fast as it runs in. When you're forty you won't have any character lines at all, if this goes on.'

'Please . . .' Georgina said. 'If you won't think of me, think of yourself. You'll be ruined too. Think of that . . .'

Maddy started writing again. 'If not this ruin, another ruin,' she said.

'You'll lose your job at the Institute!' Georgina said. 'You don't think they'll let you stay around after this . . . you could seduce a student or something!'

Maddy looked at her blandly. 'There are some results that outweigh all risk.'

Georgina put her brush down carefully on the night table next to the bed. She got up and stood for a moment looking down at Maddy's active ballpoint. She walked over to the bureau and found a cigarette amid the litter on top. She lit it. She walked over to the window overlooking the cul-de-sac and pulled back the dusty curtain and looked out. Then she went over to the bathroom door and stared through it for a moment at the toilet. She came back to the bed and sat down. Maddy stopped writing and looked at her. 'You seem a little nervous,' she said.

'You want to punish me,' Georgina said. 'I thought you were above things like that.'

'Did you?' Maddy said. 'Maybe I am. It's hard to know in situations like this. One's motives are so complex.'

'I think your motives are very simple,' Georgina said. 'You just want to do me in, because I got engaged to Haluk. You're just a vindictive lesbian.'

Maddy chewed the end of her ballpoint for a few seconds. 'What are you then?' she said.

'Me?' Georgina said.

'You got yourself engaged to Haluk Bey because you thought I'd run off to Gunzel. What's that make you?'

'I got engaged to Haluk because he's a wonderful guy and he needs me!' Georgina said.

'Sure,' Maddy said. She started writing again.

'Listen,' Georgina said. 'I'm perfectly normal. That's why I want Haluk.'

'Oh, perfectly,' Maddy said, bent over the notebook.

'This business with you was just an aberration. You know that. We were just thrown together at the Institute, like men in jail. Men in jail do that all the time.'

'Hungry animals in the State Pen,' Maddy said.

'I'm not going to let you make something nasty out of it. Just because I was fond of you.'

'I'll try to keep the nasty bits under control,' Maddy said. 'I'll try to make the whole thing uplifting.'

'Millions of people have experiences like this . . . look at all those men in the Army! It doesn't mean a thing. All psychology texts say that.'

'I know,' Maddy said. 'And of course they're right.'

'We never had a satisfactory love relationship!' Georgina said, her voice going up a register.

'God, now, that's true,' Maddy said.

'If I hadn't been perfectly normal, we would have had a satisfactory love relationship!' Georgina said.

'Was that the reason . . .' Maddy said.

'Listen!' Georgina stood up. 'You know damn well I can't enjoy sex with a woman. You've been telling me that for months, remember? Now, why do you think I can't enjoy it?'

Maddy put her pen down and sighed. 'Georgina honey, nobody enjoys sex if she's watching herself from somewhere up around the chandelier, through her grandmother's gold-rimmed glasses. That's just elementary.'

'I knew you'd try that!' Georgina said.

'Did you enjoy it with Haluk Bey last night?' Maddy said.

Georgina sat down again and lit a cigarette. 'It was one of the most beautiful moments of my life,' she said.

'Like your first kiss. In Michigan,' Maddy said.

Georgina looked at her coolly through clouds of smoke. 'It's really none of your business,' she said. 'Why should I talk to you about things that are beautiful to me, for God's sake. You just reduce everything to the nastiest level. You just *debase* everything . . .'

Maddy picked up her ballpoint again and continued writing. Georgina tapped her foot and picked tobacco off the end of her tongue.

'If you've got to write it all down, well then, write it!

But you don't have to spread it around – what's the sense in that?' Georgina said.

Maddy crossed out a word and wrote another one in the margin. 'Does Haluk Bey know that your love is as deep as a beauty-spot?' she said without looking up.

'You can't get *to* me anymore,' Georgina said. 'You can just stop that. You're wasting your time. I'm armoured in love.'

'Does he realize,' Maddy said, 'why you only make love in dark rooms with your eyes closed?'

'I'm impervious, I'm impervious,' Georgina said.

'If you're impervious,' Maddy said, 'you won't mind if I publish this historic document of our encounter, such as it was. Because it has great instructive value.'

Georgina crossed the chasm between the beds and sat down next to Maddy. 'Listen, Maddy,' she said. 'These were our private things, you know? Why do you want to tell everybody about our private things? I just don't understand why you want to do that – it's as though you never really cared anything for me at all . . .'

Maddy closed the notebook and clipped the ballpoint to the cover again She looked at Georgina for several moments. She smiled gently. Georgina leaned her head against Maddy's shoulder and took one of Maddy's hands in hers. 'I know you care for me,' she said softly. 'And I know you wouldn't really want to hurt me. You're just upset now.'

Maddy went on smiling gently. She removed her hand from Georgina's. 'I never did care for you, Georgina,' she said. 'I told you that from the beginning, only you never listen. It was your neck and shoulders. It was your green Hebrew eyes. It was a few things like that. If I could have found your neck on some nice young girl with exemplary character, I would have been blissful. It's one of the awful tricks of Fate that your eyes were distributed to you. God help us. But I made the best of it.'

'Jesus!' Georgina leapt up.

'I always hoped,' Maddy said, 'every minute we were together, that you might prove worthy of your neck and shoulders and your eyes and things like that. Once or twice I thought you were going to make it. Just for a minute or two you forgot about Yahweh's big cold eye and your grandma's gold-rimmed glasses and everything: you were just the pristine Georgina, the anarchic Georgina, my very own Noble Savage.' She shook her head sadly. 'But it didn't last,' she said. 'Your neck outstripped you every time. Your failure to keep pace with your shoulders is one of the saddest events of my life.'

Georgina stood in front of Maddy with clenched fists and the vein in her forehead turning purple. She looked very resolute. 'I'll say you made a pass at me and I rejected you and you're making up this story in revenge,' she said.

'People will laugh at you,' Maddy said.

'Why!' Georgina exploded.

'Because that's what everybody will expect you to say, after they read the document. And when you say it, they'll laugh. People always laugh when an expectation is fulfilled. It's relief, I guess,' Maddy said.

Georgina stood there with the vein in her forehead throbbing visibly. She made small indeterminate sounds in her throat. Slowly she grew very pale. The slant of her eyes increased. She sat down on the bed carefully, as though she might break something. She stared into her lap. Then she said: 'All right, you win.'

'Win?' Maddy said.

'I won't be engaged to Haluk. I'll give him up.'

'Your great love?' Maddy said. 'The illustrated man?'

'That's what you want, okay . . .' Georgina said. 'I'll stay with you.'

'Stay with me?' Maddy said.

'Oh come on,' Georgina said impatiently. 'That's what you want, isn't it? Don't act so surprised.'

Maddy let the suitcase crash onto the floor. It burst open and a pair of black panties tumbled out. She put the notebook on the night table and lit a cigarette. She leaned back on the bed and blew a smoke-ring towards the pea-green ceiling. 'I don't want you any more,' she said. 'I told you that earlier today, from the bath-tub.'

'But you couldn't . . .' Georgina said.

Maddy lowered her chin a little and looked at Georgina. 'Even though I did say it earlier, I still get the same thrill of delight up my spine when I repeat it.' She looked at the ceiling again. 'The madness is over. I could weep with joy.'

'Okay,' Georgina said. 'What *do* you want?'

'Nothing,' Maddy said. 'From you – nothing.'

'And you're going to publish that thing' – she gestured towards the notebook on the night table – 'out of spite . . .'

'Not out of spite,' Maddy said. 'Out of pride.' She sat up in the bed. 'Look, World, I have come through! No insanity is everlasting! Even necks and shoulders must come to dust! That message is my gift to the world. The world is crying for it.'

'You're out of your mind,' Georgina said.

Maddy got off the bed and stretched luxuriously. She smiled a newborn smile. She picked up the notebook and placed it carefully in her suitcase and then locked the suitcase with a miniscule key and put the key into the change purse of her handbag. 'I think I'll go have a drink,' she said. 'I feel like celebrating.'

'A drink with whom?' Georgina glowered.

'Oh, I don't know. Whoever's around – or maybe

nobody at all. Nobody would be nice. I'm too ecstatic for small talk.'

'It's Gunzel, isn't it?' Georgina said.

Maddy knelt and picked up the black panties that had spilled out of the suitcase and dropped them on the bed. 'You are as predictable as gravity,' she said.

'Well, isn't it Gunzel?' Georgina said. 'She's had her eye on you for months, don't think I haven't noticed. All that My Dear Maddy routine . . . and clutching at you. And crying! Jesus, the crying that's gone on . . .'

'Gunzel has reason to cry,' Maddy said. 'Unlike me.'

Georgina leaned forward against her knees with her head down as though she were searching for a hairpin on the carpet. But she stayed that way a long while and Maddy noticed that her head was immobile and decided she wasn't searching for something after all.

'What's wrong with you?' Maddy said.

'I think I'm going to faint,' Georgina said from between her knees.

Maddy brought a wet towel from the bathroom. She parted Georgina's hair in the back and slapped the towel across her neck. Georgina groaned and fell back on the bed. She was the colour of library dust. 'I can't take all this,' she said.

Maddy leaned over and studied the pulse in the hollow of Georgina's neck. It beat very grandly, sending little waves out from its concavity. She had her eyes clamped shut to ward off danger.

'I thought you liked an active life,' Maddy said. 'Lots of things happening . . .'

'Maybe I'm getting old,' Georgina said. 'I'm not up to it anymore.'

'Maybe it's just that the kind of things happening are not what you had in mind,' Maddy said. She wrestled the towel from behind Georgina's head and laid it across her forehead. 'Maybe life is slipping away from your tight little hands.'

'Just leave me alone,' Georgina said. She pressed the wet towel to her temples. 'Go to your new lover,' she said.

'Alas, I've no new lover,' Maddy said. 'I am poised but flight has not yet begun.'

Georgina opened her eyes. 'What's that mean exactly?' she said.

Maddy shrugged. 'Close your eyes and you'll feel better,' she said.

Georgina closed her eyes. She opened them again almost immediately. 'How will you feel when Gunzel reads that notebook? Won't you feel a little funny? I mean, this new lover reading all about her predecessor . . . all your secrets and things . . .'

'You make it sound as though we were day and night up to some dark business,' Maddy said. 'No one would think, to listen to you, that it was all as exciting as a sail on the Potomac in broad daylight.'

Georgina's lower lip trembled. 'I'm sorry you remember it that way,' she said.

'How else could I remember it, dear girl?' Maddy said.

'Maybe Gunzel will be more exciting,' Georgina said, pushing the moist towel against her eyelids. 'Maybe she'll be memorable.'

Maddy was silent. She patted Georgina perfunctorily and stood up. 'You've turned pink again,' she said. 'So I'll go and have my drink now. You have a nice rest.'

Georgina threw the towel on the floor and sat up in bed. 'I don't want to have a nice rest, damn it.'

'No?' Maddy said. 'I thought you were tired and couldn't take it any more.'

'Listen, just tell me, will you . . . just to satisfy my morbid curiosity . . . will you just tell me what you see in Gunzel? Will you just tell me that?'

Maddy thought it over. 'I don't see anything in Gunzel,' she said.

'Then who is it?' Georgina yelled. 'Because if there weren't *somebody*, you wouldn't be so calm. You'd be insulting me with every breath, you'd be calling me every name in the book, I know you. You wouldn't be taking all this lying down.'

'I didn't realize I was taking all this lying down,' Maddy said. 'I thought I'd been very vertical the whole day. There's even the possibility that I'm being vindictive. That doesn't strike me as a case of lying down. Now I just want to have a nice quiet drink, all by myself. Before I fall into bed. That's all. I just want to sit all alone in some dark foetid bar and count my blessings.'

Georgina stared at her contemptuously for a moment. 'I wasn't born yesterday, you know,' she said. 'You're up to something.'

'Just because I don't want the return of your altogether unsatisfactory person?' Maddy said.

'Oh, come *on*,' Georgina said. 'I know something's up, don't I? Last night you were mad about me, I was beautiful and adorable and you were madly in love with me and everything was coming up roses and now tonight you couldn't care less and you're going off and leave me in this condition – sick like this – and have a drink – yeah, have a drink – and you want me to believe there's nobody else . . .'

'You forgot to mention,' Maddy said, 'that in the interim you announced your engagement. You'd be surprised how things like that kill passion, for an old-fashioned girl like me. Even without a new lover.'

'So you admit there's somebody else!' Georgina said triumphantly.

'I don't know why I talk to you at all,' Maddy said. 'It's too much to expect you to get the gist of the simplest declarative sentence.'

'Last night you said –' Georgina began.

'Don't go on,' Maddy said. 'Don't say any more about last night. It makes me unbelievably nostalgic.' She stood in the middle of the floor smiling tenderly, then she lit a cigarette and walked to the door of the room. 'From one night to the next night . . .' she said, turning at the door and looking back at Georgina on the bed. 'That's quick for a compulsion to die. I feel a little bereft really. I was almost comfortable with this one, the way I'd be with an old miserable friend. Now it's gone and I feel as though the church has closed its doors and I've been locked outside.' Georgina sat propped up in bed like an unclad stone figure, staring at Maddy.

'Maybe I'm through with that,' Maddy said. 'Maybe you're the first and last of my obligatory ordeals.'

She went out of the door and closed it quietly behind her. As she walked down the hallway, she heard the door open again. But no one spoke.

At ten minutes past two Hasan Bey drew up in front of the Anadolu Palas in a Ford Anglia so old it still had running-boards. Maddy was in the dining room drinking tea and watching the street through the span of unwashed glass window. She remained seated while Hasan Bey got out of the Ford Anglia and stood by the front fender for a moment smoothing down his jacket and hitching up his trousers. He glanced at the Anadolu Palas with a pre-occupied expression. Then he started for the door. Maddy sipped the last of her tea and lit a cigarette. She felt omnipotent, as though she had just been born from the forehead of Zeus early that morning. She also felt as though her head was inside a small electric motor that had somehow stalled so that it hummed loudly and grew hot. That would be, she thought, the result of the innumerable brandies of the night before. Her celebratory brandies. It would probably be best if she turned the little motor off before it burned out its parts. But the omnipotent section of her brain refused to consider it.

Hasan Bey crossed the dining room to Maddy's table, smiling broadly – all his long white teeth glittering.

'Sweetling!' he said. 'You are looking very wonderful today.'

'I suppose that's possible,' Maddy said. 'Would you like some tea?'

'We will have something to drink on the Other Side,' he said. 'Something much better than tea.'

Maddy got up slowly and preceded him out of the dining room. Was she wobbling? There was no way to know. She had moved into another area and taken all her points of reference with her.

On the way around the Bay of Izmir Hasan Bey chattered away happily, occasionally leaning over to pat Maddy's arm, his eyes fixed on the road. She was silent. She felt a smile on her face. It had a will of its own. She wondered if it looked diabolic. Could Hasan Bey discriminate between diabolic smiles and whatever the other kind looked like? She doubted it. She felt it was probably safe to allow her face its own way, whatever it might be.

The Ford Anglia laboured up the hillside and stopped on a small plateau amid the rocks. Hasan Bey sighed with satisfaction and closed his eyes for a moment, ecstatically.

'Is the air here not very marvellous?' he said.

Maddy opened the door and stuck her feet out. 'I don't see any café,' she said.

Hasan Bey opened his eyes. 'We must walk a little more up,' he said.

Maddy got out of the car and gazed upwards. There was a little rocky path leading to a wider plateau above.

She could see some tables up there. She caught sight of the tops of two heads. Gunzel and Melek? Were they already here? She started up the hillside. Hasan Bey locked up the Ford Anglia and hurried after her. When he caught up with her he said: 'You go very fast, like a Russian girl I once knew. She was a very marvellous athlete.'

'Really,' Maddy said, concentrating on reaching the plateau before the electric motor in possession of her head spluttered into silence. At the same time, she felt quite sure she could fly to the top if she chose. It was a strange sensation.

There were three people seated at the crude wooden tables scattered across the grassy plateau: a man and a woman who stared morosely into their glasses of raki (they did not speak to each other, they did not look at the view) and an old man who looked very tired and did not seem to be eating or drinking anything at all. He appeared to be studying his feet. Hasan Bey led Maddy to a table near the stone wall at the edge of the plateau.

'From here we will have a very marvellous view of the Bay,' he said.

Maddy sat down on the wooden bench next to the table. Hasan Bey sat down across from her. After a moment a dark little man wearing an apron appeared at the end of the table. Hasan Bey spoke to him in Turkish. The little aproned figure nodded and left. Maddy looked out over the Bay of Izmir. She thought the dung-coloured speck in the distance, on the other side, was probably the Anadolu Palas. She didn't care whether it was but she thought it probably looked like that from where she was now: like a little dirty spot on her cornea.

The dark little man reappeared with a large tray on which there were two glasses, a bottle of Turkish cognac and a platter of tomatoes, yellow cheese and thick slices

of white bread that looked as though they had been violently hand-grappled from the loaf. Hasan Bey poured
the glasses full of cognac and took a large swallow from
his immediately. He seemed indifferent to the platter of
food. Maddy bit into a tomato. It was sweet and very
juicy. The pips ran down her chin. She wiped them off
with a piece of bread and drank down half her brandy in
one gulp, her eyes watering furiously.

'You will be drunk very soon if you drink the Turkish
cognac like that,' Hasan Bey said happily.

'That's true,' Maddy said. She nibbled at a chunk of
yellow cheese and tried to suppress the rage of delirious
laughter that kept rising in her throat. It was the omnipotence, she thought. She could rise up this very instant
and by strength of her indomitable will alone make that
lachrymose couple sing for joy over their raki glasses,
make that old vacant shoe-studier a darling of the gods.
She knew she could. Yes. If there were a train thundering
down upon them across the plateau, she could rise and
put her arm out against the cow-catcher and stop it dead
in its steamy tracks. Yes. Of course. It was such a day.

When Gunzel and Melek appeared at the top of the
path and stepped on to the plateau, Maddy stared at
them for a moment and then turned to Hasan Bey, who
was refilling his glass.

'Stunning blonde girl, don't you think?' she said.

Hasan Bey looked over at the two women. Gunzel was
wobbling badly on her high heels and clutching Melek's
arm to keep herself upright. She avoided Maddy's eyes.
Melek's expression was grimly embarrassed. She looked
at the ground and listened to Gunzel whispering nervously
into her ear. They sat down very primly at a table a little
distance from Maddy and Hasan Bey.

'I once knew a Norwegian girl who had hair that
colour,' Hasan Bey said.

'Yes, well, I imagine she's back in Norway now,' Maddy said. 'Isn't she.'

'Oh yes,' Hasan Bey said. 'Our meeting was very brief.'

'I should imagine.'

Hasan Bey looked momentarily melancholy at the recollection of his brief Norwegian girl. Then he snapped into the present again and poured more cognac into Maddy's glass.

'You drink like a man,' he said admiringly.

'Very thirsty women drink that way too,' Maddy said, watching Gunzel lean across the table and speak very fiercely to Melek. She could tell from the tight arch of Gunzel's shoulders that she was speaking fiercely. And from Melek's downcast and miserable face. Maddy sighed. Why did omnipotence never find an answering echo in its environment?

'I know the brunette girl,' Maddy said. 'She works in Istanbul.'

'Oh?' Hasan Bey said, looking over at Gunzel. 'She's very thin,' he said appraisingly.

'Her friend is less thin,' Maddy said. 'Really rather voluptuous.'

'Voluptuous?' Hasan Bey said, staring at Melek as though she were diseased in a way he hadn't noticed.

'I mean, she's very shapely. You know. Shapely?'

'Ah yes.' He smiled, relieved. He looked at Melek again. 'That is a very nice word. I must remember it. Voluptuous,' he repeated. 'Yes. She is very voluptuous.'

'And remarkably blue eyes,' Maddy said. 'I noticed the blue eyes as they passed our table. You don't often see a girl so amazingly photogenic, do you?'

Hasan Bey picked up the cognac bottle and refilled his glass again, studying Melek. 'Photogenic . . .' he murmured.

'Maybe she's an actress,' Maddy said. 'She could be,

with that blonde hair and those blue eyes.'

Hasan Bey mulled this over, kneading a piece of yellow cheese. 'She could be an actress,' he finally agreed. 'She has a very wonderful face. And she is voluptuous.'

'Oh yes,' Maddy said. 'Completely.' She ate another tomato, watching Hasan Bey make mental calculations. He is fitting her into his album now. He is testing her for appropriateness. He is discovering the need for a voluptuous blue-eyed blonde to complete his life's work. People with simple-minded obsessions always end up victimized. But perhaps they don't notice. Or they call it something else.

'Perhaps you should greet your friend from Istanbul,' Hasan Bey said. 'Perhaps you would like to extend that courtesy.' He shrugged, sipping his cognac. 'If you like.'

Maddy considered. 'Yes. I suppose I should do that,' she said. 'It seems the nice thing to do, doesn't it? Perhaps I should go over and speak to my friend and ask her and *her* friend to join us for a drink. Would you mind if I did that?'

'Of course not,' Hasan Bey said, smiling magnanimously. 'It would be a courtesy.'

'Fine,' Maddy said, getting up. 'I'll be right back.'

She walked over to Gunzel and Melek and stood next to their table with her back to Hasan Bey.

'Everything's going like clockwork,' she said, patting Gunzel's shoulder.

Gunzel smiled up at her tremulously, her eyes glistening.

'Now, don't start weeping, for God's sake,' Maddy said.

'I'm so nervous,' Gunzel said, blinking.

'There's nothing to be nervous about,' Maddy said. 'We've got everything going like a well-oiled machine.' She looked at Melek, who was staring at the table with her lower lip pushed out. 'Don't pout, Melek,' Maddy said. 'Look bored, that's all right. But don't pout. It spoils your photogenic face. You must above all look photogenic. Gunzel told you what to say?' Melek nodded, drawing her lower lip in. 'Good,' Maddy said. 'I'm throwing the ball to you. It's touchdown time.'

Gunzel's mouth fell open. 'I don't understand.'

'It's just a figure of speech,' Maddy said. 'Come with me.'

Gunzel and Melek arose as though on their way to the cart that would convey them to the guillotine. Gunzel took a deep shaky breath, threw back her shoulders and took Melek firmly by the arm. Melek turned very red in the face and looked as though she would burst into tears. Gunzel pinched her elbow. 'You just remember the village, my girl!' she hissed.

The three of them made their way back to where Hasan Bey sat posing with his cognac, half-profile against the clear blue sky. He smiled dazzlingly and stood up.

'Ah . . . your friends,' he said, bowing slightly. 'I am very honoured.'

Gunzel shook hands. Melek's face had gone mercifully vacant. They all sat down. Hasan Bey grandly ordered another bottle of cognac and offered his Turkish filter-tips all around. Gunzel made clouds of smoke that almost enveloped the table in minutes.

'Inhaling helps that,' Maddy said, coughing a little.

'What?' Gunzel said, tapping her ash off before it could properly grow.

'You are visiting Izmir for the first time?' Hasan Bey said to Melek, smiling his most winning smile.

Melek looked at Gunzel for a moment through her shroud of smoke. 'I am very rich and live in France,' she said.

116

Gunzel groaned and slumped against her elbow. Hasan Bey looked at her, concerned.

'Are you not well, mademoiselle?'

'It's nothing serious,' Gunzel said, lighting another cigarette from a fragment of the first. 'Melek, you shouldn't drink any cognac. It doesn't agree with you.'

Hasan Bey, who was pouring tumblers of the cognac for all, stopped with the bottle in mid-air. 'Melek?' he said. 'Melek is a Turkish name . . .'

'Mademoiselle Melek *is* Turkish,' Gunzel said. 'But it happens that she lives in France most of the time now.' She paused and puffed her filter-tip wildly for a moment. 'It happens that she is bored to live only in this country. And of course since she need not worry about . . . cost . . .'

'Ah . . . I see,' Hasan Bey said, resuming the pouring. He set the bottle down. He shrugged charmingly. 'Who would live all his time in one country?' he said.

'Quite,' Maddy said, sipping her brandy.

Hasan Bey turned to Melek. 'Always I have said that French girls are the most wonderful girls in the universe.'

'She's Turkish,' Maddy said quietly.

'Of course she is Turkish,' Hasan Bey said. 'But she *lives* in France!' he finished triumphantly.

'That explains everything,' Maddy said.

'Ah, France . . .' Hasan Bey said. '*La belle France*! It must be that you miss it when you are away, Mademoiselle Melek.'

Melek looked at him blankly, then at Gunzel. Then she nodded. 'Yes,' she said.

'Your family, they live in Izmir?' he said.

'They live in a village in the south,' Gunzel said. 'They have olive groves.'

Hasan Bey listened to Gunzel and looked at Melek. It was as though he was getting a simultaneous translation.

'Olive groves . . .' he said softly. 'That is very marvellous.'

'Olive groves can be the source of much pleasure,' Maddy said.

Hasan Bey turned and looked at her with a preoccupied air. 'You said something, sweetling?'

'I said, we have exhausted the tomatoes. Would you care to order more?'

'Tomatoes . . .' he said. 'Yes. Of course.'

He ordered another platter of food.

'Do you like to dance, Mademoiselle Melek?' he said.

'No,' Melek said.

'How can you lie so!' Gunzel screeched. 'You know you cannot get enough dancing ever to satisfy your soul.'

Melek stared at Gunzel and then smiled wanly at Hasan Bey. 'I cannot get enough dancing ever to satisfy my soul,' she said. 'Excuse me for lying.'

Gunzel leaned more heavily against the wooden table. She fingered an unlit cigarette. She looked at Maddy and shook her head slowly from side to side. Hasan Bey went on gazing at Melek with a fixed smile. He seemed oblivious of the others.

'Have some cheese, Gunzel,' Maddy said. 'Let the air clear a bit.'

'The rhumba?' Hasan Bey said to Melek.

'Anyone who can't get enough dancing ever to satisfy her soul would naturally love the rhumba,' Maddy said.

'I love the rhumba,' Melek said. She sat with her hands folded in her lap. She did not touch the cognac.

'Wonderful!' Hasan Bey exclaimed. 'Very very wonderful.' He poured everyone another glass of cognac in celebration of his discovery. Except for Melek, whose glass was full. 'You do not drink your brandy, Mademoiselle Melek . . .' he said, reproachfully.

'She drinks only French cognac,' Gunzel said. Having finished her yellow cheese, she was stuffing tomatoes into her mouth, one after the other, very quickly. 'Only the very best French cognac.'

Hasan Bey looked down miserably at the bottle in his hand, set it down and sighed. 'If I still was working for NATO, I would buy the best French cognac. It was always for sale at the PX. It was a very wonderful thing to see.'

Gunzel shrugged. 'It is unimportant,' she said. 'Mademoiselle Melek will soon have all the French cognac she wishes.'

'She is leaving soon?' Hasan Bey asked in alarm.

'When she chooses to,' Gunzel said languorously. 'Who can know when that will be?'

'Perhaps you can persuade Mademoiselle Melek not to return to France right away, Hasan,' Maddy said. 'What a shame to lose such a lovely dancing-partner.' She lit a cigarette, now that Gunzel's fog had lifted.

'Yes, yes!' Hasan Bey said fervently. He grasped Melek's hand. Melek's mouth flew open. 'I shall not let this very wonderful girl rush away to France!' He smiled at her overwhelmingly. 'You would like to stay in Izmir a while, would you not, Mademoiselle? To have a dance with Hasan?' he added, in his most seductive tone.

Melek sat frozen, staring at Hasan Bey's hands, which enclosed her own. Her mouth remained limply open. She seemed powerless to move. Gunzel was transfixed, a tomato poised before her lips. There was an increase in the volume of sound from the small electric motor which contained Maddy's head. How could it escape everyone's attention? But no one seemed to notice. All in fact were hanging on the mute Melek, hypnotized by the sight of that soundless open mouth.

'Eh, Mademoiselle Melek . . .?' Hasan Bey urged. 'You will stay in Izmir a while . . .?'

'Melek . . .' Gunzel began, dropping the tomato back on to the platter. 'Have you lost your tongue?'

Melek shook her head. She continued to stare at Hasan Bey's hairy knuckles, which lay on the table just in front of her.

'I should imagine . . .' Maddy said, 'that Mademoiselle Melek can do whatever –' She stopped suddenly. Melek extricated her hand from the basket of Hasan Bey's grip and with that same hand she grasped the full glass of cognac sitting before her and in one motion finished it off.

Gunzel placed both her hands palm down on the table and stretched her body upwards to its full sitting height. 'What are you *doing*!' she screamed. 'You will be sick.'

'No,' Melek said stubbornly, dropping her hands back into her lap. The negative sounded to Maddy like a general and all-embracing one.

Hasan Bey lifted the cognac bottle with a smile and started in the direction of Melek's now-empty glass. 'So after all Mademoiselle Melek will drink Turkish cognac.'

Gunzel grasped the bottle and set it down again, still attached to Hasan Bey's arm. 'You will not give her any more brandy,' she said. 'I forbid it.'

'*You* forbid it, mademoiselle . . .?' Hasan Bey said. 'Are you the guardian of this lady?'

'She will be sick,' Gunzel said. 'She cannot drink without being sick. Do you want that to happen? Are you such a man?'

Hasan Bey meditated, looking yearningly at Melek, who sat with her hands folded again in her lap. She looked like a stone figure – except that her mouth (closed at last) was curved in a very slight, almost imperceptible smile. Maddy laughed, hoping it would be brief.

'Sweetling,' Hasan Bey turned to her, distracted. 'It is not a thing to laugh about.'

'I know, I know,' Maddy said, laughing. 'It is a tragedy.'

'Dear God . . .' Gunzel said. She lit another of Hasan Bey's filter-tips.

'You mean,' Hasan Bey addressed his interpreter, Gunzel, 'that the Mademoiselle cannot even drink champagne? How does she amuse herself while she is dancing?'

Gunzel regarded him speechlessly through the renewed curtain of smoke.

'How can you ask such a question, Hasan,' Maddy said. 'You, a Man of the World.'

Hasan Bey struggled to decipher this.

'Champagne is a childish pastime,' Maddy said. She moulded a piece of yellow cheese into an ellipse. She concentrated on this.

Hasan Bey looked uncertain and then slowly his consternation faded and a smile crept onto his face. He lowered his heavy eyelids and peered lasciviously at Melek through the liquid slits. He chuckled softly.

Maddy bit her cheese-ellipse in two and swallowed half of it.

Melek went on smiling.

'It's time we were on our way,' Maddy said. She stood up.

'You wish to go?' Hasan Bey said.

'I wish to go,' Maddy said. 'Back to the Anadolu Palas. Back to the other side of the Other Side. Are you in a car?' she asked Gunzel.

'We came by taxi,' Gunzel said.

'Then Hasan Bey will take you back. Won't you, Hasan?'

Hasan Bey collected himself. 'If you will allow me, ladies . . . it will be a pleasure,' he said, getting up and bowing all at the same time, which was an awkward business.

Gunzel inclined her head as though accepting fate. 'Mademoiselle Melek is staying with me in my apartment during this visit. You could drop us there, please. Get up, Melek. We are going now.'

Melek stood up. Her arms hung limply at her sides. She continued to smile her almost-imperceptible smile.

'I would be honoured if all you ladies would have dinner with me tonight,' Hasan Bey said. 'I know a very marvellous fish restaurant, on the Bay.'

'That's a splendid suggestion!' Maddy said. 'I can't make it myself but I'm sure the other ladies would find it irresistible.'

'Irresistible,' Gunzel repeated weakly. 'Move, Melek – we are going down the hill now.'

Hasan Bey excused himself and went over to speak to the little dark man in the apron, who stood at the entrance to the small serving-tent at the back of the plateau. There was a lengthy exchange. At one point Hasan grasped the little man feelingly by one shoulder. Shortly thereafter he offered him a filter-tip. The little man looked at him expressionlessly for a moment and then took out of his pocket a pad of paper and a pencil and began writing. Occasionally, without looking up from his pad, he said something to Hasan, who put his head back and closed his eyes for a moment, reckoning – and then replied. When the little man was through writing, he handed the pad to Hasan, who propped it against his knee and signed it.

During this interchange at the serving-tent, Gunzel was speaking rapidly, in a low intense voice, to Melek, who continued to smile vaguely out over the Bay of Izmir.

'You must collect yourself, Melek. Stop this silly smiling and collect yourself. We are going in the car with this man in only a few minutes. You must speak to him now and then. You must say something. You cannot act like a sheep in the fields. Is that not so, Maddy?'

'That is so,' Maddy said. 'You must pull yourself together, Melek, my dear girl. Even Hasan Bey will eventually notice that you are speechless and immobile. He will wonder how you could ever conceivably dance the rhumba. It will be a fatal question.'

'You must try to act sensibly,' Gunzel said. 'Try to act as if you have good sense. Maddy and I know you have got no sense at all. But you must act! Do you hear me!'

'The world is full of people pretending to have good sense and making a decent show of it,' Maddy said. 'You could be one of those. But you must try harder. Effort is all! Are you listening?'

Melek smiled and looked into the fair blue sky.

'Is she conscious?' Maddy said. 'You know her better than I do.'

Gunzel studied Melek's face intently. 'I cannot swear to it,' she groaned. 'I have never seen her like this. It is a new condition.'

'As long as Hasan Bey thinks she's conscious . . .' Maddy said. 'He requires very little evidence in these matters.'

'I am very worried,' Gunzel said. 'How can we go to a fish restaurant like this? I don't know what she will say to him. She might do something!'

'On the other hand,' Maddy said, 'she might do nothing at all – neither speak nor move. That would be worse. Hasan likes lots of twirling and self-expression.'

'Dear God,' Gunzel said, grasping Melek's arm. 'How did it come to this . . .'

'Have courage,' Maddy said. She looked at Melek for a moment, considering. 'What's really worrying is this sudden display of rebelliousness. This independent decision to drink down all that cognac, despite your instructions. Is Melek struggling into maturity, do you suppose?'

'Dear God,' Gunzel repeated, putting her hand to her

forehead. 'Have I not had troubles enough in my life?'

Hasan returned from the serving-tent, smiling expectantly. 'We will go now, ladies,' he said. He held out his arm for Melek. 'Mademoiselle . . .'

Melek turned her head slowly away from the horizon. She looked at Hasan Bey, her vague smile becoming more focused. 'I am very rich and live in France,' she said sweetly. 'Among the olive groves. I cannot get enough dancing ever to satisfy my soul. Most especially do I like to dance the rhumba . . . in the . . . olive groves.' She faltered, then found the strength to continue, smiling at Hasan Bey beatifically. 'I am very photographic,' she concluded.

When Maddy got back to the Anadolu Palas just before five o'clock there was a letter from Georgina waiting for her at the desk. The pink envelope was scented and there was a small cerise flower in the lower left corner. Maddy looked at the envelope for a minute, feeling extremely tired, and then went upstairs to the pea-green room and sat down on the side of her bed and opened it. The paper inside was even more noticeably scented. It made Maddy feel a little bilious.

'Dear Maddy [the letter read], After last night it's pretty clear that we have nothing else to say to each other, except goodbye. I've never been so disappointed in anyone in my life. I suppose as the years pass I'll get over the hurt. I'm sorry you can't understand what I've been going through lately. Anyway, I want you to know that I'll always think of you fondly, even if you do publish that awful notebook of yours. I can't find it in my heart to be vindictive, regardless. I'll try to keep out of your way at the Institute. I certainly don't want to be anywhere I'm not wanted. Love, Georgina. P.S. I've moved into Haluk's apt. I'll see you at the airport Sunday night.

P.P.S. I hope you and Gunzel will be very happy.'

Maddy lay back across the bed and closed her eyes. She had expected to feel rejuvenated after a short holiday in Izmir. She had needed a rest from the Institute, a change of scene. A change of scene had always done wonders for her in the past. Now she felt forty years old and at the end of her tether. Drained of her life's blood. Would she have the strength to reach the airport in two days? It seemed a task equivalent to scaling Everest. How could she face the two months until the Christmas recess? She would stand in front of her class of eager little Turkish girls and open her mouth and nothing would come out but a warm, expiring breath. She had been fighting tiredness for a decade. Perhaps she would quit fighting it now and relax into the final fatigue. She was only twenty-seven. Perhaps she need not struggle beyond thirty. The thought of it made her smile serenely.

She fell asleep and woke up at six o'clock. The room felt peculiarly vacant without Georgina. The maid had been in to clean and straighten and dust. She had pushed Maddy's suitcase under the bed. There was no evidence that anyone was there. It was as though she had wandered into an unoccupied hotel room, to sleep illicitly on a bed that wasn't hers. She got up and went into the bathroom. She was relieved to see her toothbrush and toothpaste on the shelf above the handbasin. She *was* still there, after all.

She thought how strange it was that people miss even the pain in their lives. Anything they can gather to themselves – even thorns, thistles and wounds – they cherish. It's all evidence that they are there, that they haven't vanished. Screaming and weeping are ontological activities.

I am going to be sick, she thought. There is this queer awareness of breathing and metabolism. I can feel my kidneys siphoning off the bile. My toenails growing. It is all unnatural, a harbinger of disintegration. Shall I lie down and prepare myself?

There was a knock on the door.

'Go away!' Maddy yelled.

There was a moment's silence and then another knock.

'I said, go away! I am not at home to anyone.'

'Dear God . . .' Gunzel said in a small weak voice from the other side of the door.

Maddy opened the door and glared at her. 'I've done all I can do,' she said. 'Absolutely all. I'm finished. Don't ask.'

'Please . . .' Gunzel leaned against the door-frame.

'Come in. But don't expect anything. I've retired from the field. I've shot my bolt.'

Gunzel came in and slumped down on the bed. She rubbed her hands across her face as though she was doubtful it was all in one piece. 'I am at the end of my rope,' she said.

Maddy lit a cigarette and sat down on the other bed, waiting, feeling some sort of unidentifiable process at work in her stomach.

'Melek has disappeared into thin air,' Gunzel said, incredulous.

'In an hour?' Maddy said.

'In an hour. Yes. In one hour.'

'I don't believe it,' Maddy said. 'Why should she disappear? Where would she disappear *to*? Maybe she just wandered off for a minute. Maybe she's sitting in some unlikely place, knitting.'

'She left a note,' Gunzel said.

'That seems the fashionable thing to do these days.'

'Pardon?'

'What was in the note?' Maddy said.

Gunzel opened her handbag and extracted a crumpled

piece of ruled students' paper. She handed it to Maddy.

It read: 'I do not wish to marry this man with the thick eyes. He has fingers with hairs on them, his chest also has hairs. I like smooth men, without hairs except on their heads. Do not be angry with me. I cannot marry a man with such hairs. I go away now. Love, Melek.'

Maddy handed the ruled sheet back to Gunzel and they sat silently looking at each other across the little space between the beds.

'Well, after all,' Maddy said, 'it's just as good a reason for not marrying someone as anything else I've heard of. In fact, it's a lot more basic than refusing to marry a man because his bank account's too small. If more women refused to marry men with hairs on their fingers – maybe the world would be a happier place.'

Gunzel looked puzzled. 'I don't understand you some-times,' she said.

'It's not important,' Maddy said.

'What shall I do?' Gunzel wailed, her eyes beginning to leak. 'Hasan Bey is coming to collect us at seven o'clock.'

'Tell him Mademoiselle Melek chose this very evening to return to France. Say she is an unpredictable girl and he is better off with someone poor and hampered in her movements.'

'Ah, dear God, have I not had troubles enough –'

'Shut up that bawling,' Maddy said. 'I'm sick of all you weeping women. Isn't there a joyful ruthless dry-eyed woman anywhere in creation?'

Gunzel wiped her eyes on a lace handkerchief and stared at Maddy. 'Are you not well?' she said.

'You ask that as though it were a simple thing to answer,' Maddy said. 'I thought it was curtains just a few minutes ago, but in these transitional periods it's hard to tell sometimes.'

Gunzel shook her head sadly and dabbed at her eyes. 'I think Georgina has made you angry with all of us. But we are not all Georginas. Some of us are nice.'

'I am not angry with all of you. I am tired. I am very, very tired. Tell Hasan Bey she has disappeared into thin air, as all rich eccentrics do from time to time. Tell him to look for another dancing-partner. At the same time, kindly tell him not to call on me again. Tell him I have the plague.'

'Could I have a cigarette?' Gunzel said.

Maddy handed her a cigarette and lit it for her. Then she went over and opened the window overlooking the cul-de-sac. 'Try to blow the smoke this way,' she said. 'Let it drift out to sea.'

'I am very sad,' Gunzel said, letting out a great mouthful of smoke. 'What will become of Melek? What will become of *me*?'

'God knows,' Maddy said. She got up and opened the bottom drawer of the bureau and found the slight remains of a bottle of orange liqueur she had bought the second day in Izmir. She took the cork out and drank two large swallows from the bottle.

'I have never seen you do that before,' Gunzel said. 'You are upset, I think.'

'There are a great many things you've never seen me do which nevertheless I do quite regularly,' Maddy said. 'I drink straight booze from a bottle whenever I feel the need for a direct infusion. It's quite common for me to feel such a need in Izmir.'

Gunzel watched her, considering. 'You don't like it here, that makes me very sad. I wanted you to like it here.'

Maddy was silent, studying the label on the orange liqueur bottle. She had another swallow. 'Where do you suppose she's gone?' she said. 'Back to the village?'

'God help us,' Gunzel said, puffing away.

'Where else?' Maddy said. 'Somewhere in Izmir?'

'She has probably fallen into the hands of some slaver by this time,' Gunzel said grimly. 'Slavers are always looking for blonde girls. She will probably end up in Cairo, in the harem of some rich, filthy merchant.'

'Perhaps she won't notice,' Maddy said. 'But will the slaver not object to getting two for the price of one?'

Gunzel held her head. 'Dear God, who knows?'

'Are you going to search for her?' Maddy said. 'Or just call it a day?'

'I feel I should lie down and rest,' Gunzel said. 'Melek has exhausted me.'

'Maybe she'll turn up unexpectedly.'

'Everything Melek does is unexpected, because she has no reason for anything she does,' Gunzel said. 'She has not even a *hidden* reason. She is like a little stupid goat, except that she knits.'

'Have a drink,' Maddy said. She handed the bottle over. Gunzel took it, looked at it speculatively for several moments, and then gulped down an enormous mouthful. She coughed a good deal afterwards and her eyes watered.

'Are you going to see Hasan Bey at seven?' Maddy said. 'Or simply disappear into thin air like your friend?'

'I don't know,' Gunzel said miserably. 'What do you think I should do?'

'I'm through thinking for today.'

'Perhaps if Melek isn't there, he will become violent,' Gunzel said.

Maddy laughed until she had to sit down again.

'Why is that funny?' Gunzel said, slightly offended.

'I'm not quite finished thinking, after all,' Maddy said. 'I'll tell you a great truth. Listen closely. People who continually view themselves through a camera's eye are not inclined to be violent. To be violent you've got to be immersed in your skin – not somewhere out there with a black hood over your head and a light meter in your hand.'

'I'm sure that is a great truth,' Gunzel said. 'But I don't understand it.'

'Let's just say that I more or less guarantee you that Hasan Bey will not become violent when he discovers Melek has vanished. He will probably be very cross. But he will not be violent.'

Gunzel mulled this over after having another swallow of the orange liqueur. 'All right,' she said. 'I'll see him at seven. I'll tell him she went back to France. She just suddenly decided to return to France.' She giggled. She handed the bottle back to Maddy.

'Let me know how it all turns out,' Maddy said. She opened the door, cradling the orange liqueur bottle in the crook of her arm.

Gunzel got up and walked to the door. She stopped halfway there and looked at Maddy, chewing her lower lip. 'Dear God, I'm nervous. What will become of us all?'

'Something appropriate to our imperfections,' Maddy said. 'If things go along in a normal way.'

Maddy put the finishing touches to the record of what she referred to in her head as L'Affaire Georgina. She left several blank pages at the end of the notebook for addenda. She felt sure there would be addenda. Then she went out to walk in the streets of Izmir, feeling wonderfully alone. Feeling pristine and simple, perhaps the way Melek might say she felt (Maddy thought), if Melek could ever say such a thing.

Without Georgina at her side chattering away like a magpie, or Gunzel teetering along on her absurdly high heels – it seemed to Maddy that the very air of the city was altered. She studied the palm trees. Faces. Vehicles.

Paving-stones. New, all of it. As pristine as she was. She saw it for the first time. She had spent seven blind days in Izmir. Love was not blind in the way people said: lovers saw the beloved clearly; what they didn't see was everything else, for which they had no time.

She walked down to the Bay and along the corniche. It was a bright blue day. The sun came off the water and into Maddy's eyes like a white knife. She reeled into a small café and sat down, seeing only shadows for the first few minutes. When the waiter came into focus at her elbow, she ordered a coffee and leaned back, relaxed, turning her silver spoon over and over, looking at it as though it were the dangling object of some hypnotist. When her coffee was served, she took a sip of it, closed her eyes, and let the grainy liquid slide around her teeth and slowly down her throat. She felt she hadn't tasted coffee in seven days – longer than seven days: L'Affaire Georgina had taken her appetite for months. Stunted her taste buds. Left her coffeeless.

Suddenly she felt the presence of another, like a subtle change in the air-currents around the table. She opened her eyes. Georgina sat across from her, clutching the edge of the table as though it were a life-raft. Her eyes were rounder than Maddy had ever imagined they might be. Her eyebrows crested up around her widow's peak. She was pale. She throbbed silently like a very new motor. A dark bruise about two inches in diameter coloured her left cheek.

'I've been looking for you everywhere,' Georgina said breathlessly.

'I didn't leave a forwarding address. There was a reason for that.'

'I know how you feel, Maddy, but Jesus . . .' Georgina began.

'You don't know at all how I feel,' Maddy said. 'You

could never imagine how glorious it is since my life became unpeopled.'

'Unpeopled?' Georgina said. 'Listen, Maddy, he's as crazy as a loon. Really. I mean it. Look at my face. Just look at it!'

'I'm looking,' Maddy said.

'He's probably out right now turning the place upside down, trying to find me.' She drummed her fingers spasmodically on the table and looked over her shoulder at the door. 'I just managed to get away by the skin of my teeth. He had to go out for another bottle.'

Maddy looked at her, sipping the dregs of her coffee. 'I'm having another of these. You want one?'

'Jesus . . . how can you sit there calmly drinking coffee at a time like this?'

Maddy shrugged. 'Your maniac's not looking for me. Is he.'

Georgina looked incredulous. 'You're deserting me?' she said. 'You're just going to sit there and let this loony finish me off? Is that it?'

Maddy signalled the waiter for two more coffees. 'It all sounds like very high adventure to me.'

Georgina leaned back, resigned. 'Go ahead,' she said. 'Say whatever you want to. Say you told me so and all the rest of it. Go ahead. I don't care any more.'

'I won't bother,' Maddy said. 'It's nothing to me. I'm out of it.'

'Don't you care what happens to me?' Georgina said, sitting forward again, clutching the edge of the table again. 'You're just going to turn your back and let Haluk do me in, without lifting a finger – is that it?' The waiter set the coffee down. She picked up hers and looked into the cup and put it down again without drinking. 'You can't even be humane, is that it? Jesus . . . you'd do as much for a dog.'

'A dog wouldn't be in a spot like this,' Maddy said. 'A dog would have peed on Haluk Bey and that would have been the end of it.'

Georgina slumped in her chair, hand to her forehead. 'You've got to help me,' she said. 'If he finds me, I've had it. He's crazy, I tell you.'

'Go somewhere and hide,' Maddy said.

'Where, for God's sake?' Georgina said. 'The hotel's no good. That's the first place he'll look.'

'Gunzel's, then.'

Georgina looked down into her lap. 'I thought of that. But I can't go there without you. She probably wouldn't let me in. Not since you two are . . .'

'I do not exist in conjunction with any other pronoun,' Maddy said. 'I've given all that up.'

'Please . . .' Georgina said miserably. 'Take me over there. She'll do anything you say. She'll hide me until Sunday. That's all I ask.'

'That's all, is it?' Maddy said.

'Is that much?' Georgina screeched. 'Is that much – I ask you!'

'You are walking through my clean head with your muddy boots,' Maddy said. 'That's all. Nothing, really.'

Georgina stared at her. 'I don't get you,' she said after a minute. 'Sometimes I think you're as crazy as that nut Haluk.'

'You've no discrimination at all,' Maddy said.

'Listen, Maddy . . .' Georgina started.

'Now *you* listen,' Maddy said, setting her empty cup down. 'I'll take you over to Gunzel's and you can work out your own arrangements with her. But understand this – nothing has changed just because Haluk's proven to be a lunatic. I'm not undertaking to protect the little dogie who's just wandered home again. I'm not going to succour or sustain. I'm not going to hold your hand and tell you everything's going to be just okay. I'm not going to be your travelling nursemaid while you have the vapours all the way back to Istanbul. And we're *not* going to continue where we left off when we get back. That's all absolutely finished, as I told you before. Understand? No more. You get one more quick trip through my head – and that's it.'

Georgina looked at her, mouth open. Then she picked up her cold coffee and took a swallow and sat staring into her cup as though seeing faraway visions of things in it. She looked up at Maddy again, green eyes glistening.

'You just don't forgive anybody even one little mistake, do you? I suppose you're perfect yourself.'

'Perfect? If I were perfect I wouldn't even worry about you muddying up my head. I wouldn't even recognize the possibility. It just wouldn't exist. I'd be like Melek – I just wouldn't even notice. My frailty makes me notice.'

'Muddying up your head!' Georgina said in a strangled voice. 'Jesus . . . who do you think you are, saying a thing like that to me!' Then she recovered herself, remembering her peril. 'Okay,' she said. 'We won't discuss it now. Let's just get out of here.'

'There's nothing to discuss,' Maddy said. 'Ever again.'

'These Turkish men – they are all brutes,' Gunzel said. 'Uncivilized brutes.'

Georgina smiled wanly and lit another cigarette. 'It was all a terrible mistake,' she said. 'He was a real wolf in sheep's clothing.'

'You will stay here until we leave,' Gunzel said emphatically. 'You will be safe here. My mother will be away until Sunday morning, so there will be no one to disturb you.'

'Thank you, Gunzel,' Georgina said humbly. 'I really do appreciate this.'

Gunzel smiled magnanimously. 'Friends must take care of one another, is that not so?'

'Indeed,' Maddy said. 'Friends must rise to these occasions of menace.'

Gunzel looked at her uncertainly. Then she got up and patted Georgina on the shoulder. 'I will prepare some lunch for us now,' she said. She bustled away into the kitchen.

Maddy sat for a moment gazing at Georgina, who reclined in a roomy armchair, her head back and her eyes closed. She was the image of the martyr who could tell many stories of her persecution but who did not choose to share her sorrow. Maddy rose and went to the kitchen.

'You saw Hasan Bey last night?' she said to Gunzel.

'Oh yes,' Gunzel said, washing spinach at the sink. 'He was very distraught by Melek's disappearance. He seemed truly sad.'

'I'm sure he did,' Maddy said. 'Has he gone away for good now?'

Gunzel shrugged. 'You never know about people,' she said.

Maddy watched her fling the spinach into a pot. 'What does that mean?' she said.

'Oh well, he may be back, you know. You can't forbid people.'

'Can't you . . .' Maddy said. 'I always thought you could.'

Gunzel turned the fire on under the spinach. She put a quantity of yogurt into a saucepan. She seasoned it and turned on a very low flame. 'He is not a bad man, really,' she said. 'He seems very . . . gentle.'

'I would have said absent,' Maddy said. 'Impotent.'

Gunzel looked at her and smiled a knowing, worldly-wise smile. She stirred the yogurt.

'You are very critical,' she said. 'Westerners are so

often very critical.'

'Changing horses in midstream seems to have no national limitations, however,' Maddy said.

'Horses? I don't understand,' Gunzel said, stirring the yogurt.

'Perhaps you'll be very happy with Hasan Bey. Who knows? You'll have to tell him things too, of course. But you don't really mind that, do you?'

The spoon stopped in mid-air. 'I?' Gunzel said. 'With Hasan Bey?'

'Your new horse,' Maddy said. 'A better mount than the old, perhaps. A *new* mount, at least.'

'I only said you never know about people,' Gunzel said. 'Some are nicer than we think when we first see them. Isn't that so? That doesn't mean I will form some relationship with Hasan Bey.' She removed the top of the pot and peered in at the spinach.

'And Melek?' Maddy said.

'Oh, Melek . . .' Gunzel shrugged. 'I wash my hands of Melek. She cannot be helped. She is beyond help.' She took the spinach pot off the stove and frowned. 'She was never satisfactory, as a friend,' she said.

'If only I could get to the bottom of this word – satisfactory . . .' Maddy said. 'Have you considered Georgina? She's available now. If you have enormous patience and expect little, perhaps she will be a satisfactory friend.'

Gunzel looked shocked. 'What are you saying!' she said.

'There you both are – high and dry,' Maddy said. 'Between plays, as they say. Proximity and availability are a good beginning.'

'But you and Georgina . . .' Gunzel began.

'There is nothing between Georgina and me but the memory of a disturbance. Even that little keepsake will fade away.'

Gunzel considered this, stirring the yogurt again. 'You were . . . very fond of Georgina.'

Maddy laughed.

'You were!' Gunzel protested indignantly. '*Very* fond of Georgina . . .'

'Oh yes,' Maddy said. 'Very fond. But that's over. Nothing left but a little tremor in the water, to show that something passed by.'

Gunzel put the spoon down. 'I think you are making fun of me,' she said.

'You seem to have changed your opinion of Georgina, that's all,' Maddy said. 'Ever since her tragedy. I just thought you might like to become fast friends, now that you've gone so far as to change your opinion.'

Gunzel spread the spinach on a platter and spooned the yogurt over it. She put the saucepan and the spoon down and looked at Maddy. 'Once I thought you and I . . . could be friends. I hoped –'

'I've retired,' Maddy said.

'But you must have friends!' Gunzel said. She moved a step nearer Maddy. She extended one arm.

'I've thought about that a lot,' Maddy said, 'and I don't think I must at all.'

'I could be a good friend,' Gunzel said. 'Not like Georgina.'

'You forget things in minutes,' Maddy said. 'Just minutes, really. As though they'd never been. You do it with such ease. It baffles me. My forgetting has always been strenuous. It exhausts me. It leads me down strange anaesthetizing paths.' She paused and sat down at the little table over which Melek had bowed, weeping, a few days before. She ran her fingers over the marble surface. 'It all comes to the same thing in the end, though. Doesn't it?'

Gunzel sat down across from her, leaning forward

intently. 'I won't forget you,' she said.

'You've forgotten Melek. Already.'

Gunzel sat back, her eyes wide. 'I haven't forgotten Melek. I tell you that honestly. I am very sad and very hurt. I think it will be a long time before I recover myself from this pain.'

'But you don't mind whiling away these painful hours with me, do you?' Maddy said. 'Or with Hasan Bey. Or even with Georgina. Your grief is very convivial.'

Gunzel looked at Maddy reproachfully. 'Why do you say these things to me?'

'I don't know,' Maddy said. She lit a cigarette. 'Forgetting is so general, why should I punish you for your little bit of it? Why should I punish you because mine is hard and drives me to the brink? It's like hitting somebody because they add faster.'

Gunzel struggled with this. 'What are you saying to me?' she said.

'I'm going now,' Maddy said. 'I leave Georgina to you. I'm sure you'll hit it off. She's very flexible.'

Gunzel clutched Maddy's arm. 'Why are you going?' she said. 'We must still speak some more!'

'No more speaking,' Maddy said. 'Scratch me off your list. I'm ineligible. I'm giving up my practice.'

'Practice?' Gunzel said.

'Maybe after a few years, I'll get a whole new set of people,' Maddy said. 'After my head's been vacant for a while and I've repaired the furniture and unplugged the drains. Maybe I'll get some new tenants. I don't know. Maybe I won't. Maybe I'll fall over the brink instead. That's what brinks are for.'

'I . . .' Gunzel began.

'If you speak to Georgina now, she'll always think of you fondly. Because you saw her suffering. You can be her memory of suffering, remind her later on that she

suffered. She'll be grateful. Goodbye,' Maddy said, pushing through the kitchen door.

As she passed the living-room door on her way out, she
saw Georgina lift her head and open her eyes, startled.
'Maddy . . .?' she said. 'Is that you?'

Maddy closed the door to the apartment and went
slowly down the stairs. Shake the bottle and let us all
settle again, she thought. Float through the water – arms
stretched out and flying like flags – and settle again.

The world is ending, Maddy thought. How very noisy it
is! I always thought it would be noisy but not like this.
Not like a terrible thunder on my skull. Like a ripping in
two, that's the way I always thought it would sound. But
it sounds like someone knocking on my skull . . . She
woke up slowly and lay listening attentively. Then she
turned her head and looked at the door of the room. The
world seemed to be ending over there, after all. She got
up and opened the door and Haluk Bey exploded into the
room – all wings and beak, a thin eagle flapping around
Maddy's head, cawing angrily. The end of the world
might have been preferable, Maddy thought.

'Where is she?' he demanded. 'What have you done
with her?'

Maddy sat down on the bed again. 'As we've both
observed before, Georgina's a big girl now,' she said. 'She
walks, she talks, she goes away.'

'You have spirited her away,' he bellowed. 'I demand
to know where she is!'

'She looked a little worn after only one night,' Maddy
said. 'Imagine how used up she would have been in a
week or two.'

'Don't think you can stop me with all this talk of yours!'
Haluk Bey said. 'You're not so smart as you think.' He
leaned into Maddy's face. 'You haven't got Georgina any

139

more,' he whispered malevolently.

Maddy sighed. 'I never *had* Georgina. And you don't have her. Nobody has her. She's not haveable – like a building. Like a Trade Mart.'

Haluk Bey leaned back again, glaring at her. A dark prickly stubble covered the lower half of his face – at least two days' worth, Maddy reckoned. His suit looked as though it had been slept in wet the night before. His eyes were wine-coloured, like burgundy. The pupils looked like cigarette ash. How could a man's pupils go pale? It was remarkable.

'I will not go until I know where she is,' he said. 'We are going to be married.'

'I think Georgina's called off the engagement,' Maddy said. 'Although of course I never know how firm any of these renouncements are. I can't tell you where she is. I don't think she wants you to know. Tomorrow this may be different. Why don't you just wait around a while and see how it goes?'

Haluk Bey sat down on the other bed. His face relaxed into sarcastic rancour. 'You think you can hide her from me?' he said softly, smiling malignantly.

'The great Yahweh has hidden her from one and all,' Maddy said. 'She is pressed to His Bosom.' She lit her first cigarette of the day. 'You shouldn't have beaten her up, you know. At least for the first week or so.'

'I did not touch her,' he said.

'Someone touched her,' Maddy said. 'Did you have house-guests?'

Haluk Bey went on smiling. 'No one laid a finger on her,' he said. 'She had an accident.'

'Did she . . .'

'She fell down the stairs. She drank too much and fell down the stairs.' He shrugged. 'It was unfortunate.'

'Yes, it was,' Maddy said.

He looked around the pea-green room. 'So this is where you stay,' he said, continuing to smile unpleasantly. 'It is a very poor room for a modern Western woman.'

'It is a very poor room for a coolie,' Maddy said.

'I am surprised you stay here.'

'I don't identify with the Anadolu Palas,' Maddy said. 'I don't have personal relationships with hotel rooms.'

'No? You are too busy with your women, I suppose . . .'

'Vastly too busy,' Maddy said.

Haluk Bey lifted his eagle-beak and closed his lips over his small crooked teeth. The lips continued to suggest a smile. 'You have always a smart answer for everything,' he said.

'Silly questions I can answer straight off,' she said. 'There's nothing to that.'

'You think you have won the contest, Miss Tilson. But you have not won.'

Maddy leaned down and pulled on her bath slippers. Then she looked at Haluk Bey for a minute. 'To be a contest, there has to be a prize,' she said. 'Georgina is unawardable. Now I'd like to take a bath, if you'd be good enough to leave.'

'All American women are too smart for their own good,' he said. 'You are too smart for your own good, Miss Tilson.'

'It's too soon to say,' Maddy said, standing up. 'It really is just too soon to say.'

'Georgina will come back to me,' he said. 'She cannot stay away.'

Maddy thought about this, sucking her cigarette and studying Haluk Bey's burgundy eyes. 'It's strange to think of Georgina suffering a compulsion of that sort,' she said. 'They've always been protective in the past.'

'But I am right,' Haluk Bey said. 'You will see.'

'Tell me something,' Maddy said. 'Do I remind you of your Lost American Love?'

Haluk Bey laughed. 'You are very fanciful, Miss Tilson. I dislike you for yourself alone.'

'You're quite sure?' Maddy said. 'I wouldn't like being a substitute for some crummy American blonde.' She snuffed out her cigarette. 'Now get out, please.'

Haluk Bey sighed a parody of a sigh. 'Dear Miss Tilson, as I told you – I will not leave until you tell me where you have secreted Georgina.'

'All right,' Maddy said. 'You just make yourself comfortable, then. Perhaps you'll learn to enjoy the decor in time.'

She locked the bathroom door behind her. She wondered (drawing her bath) if he would steal her suitcase, tear her clothes into shreds, write obscene messages on the mirror with lipstick, put a lethal insect under the bedclothes, or simply lie in wait for her with a long knife in his lap. She climbed into the tub and lay back, gazing up at the sweaty ceiling.

I shall write my memoirs, she thought. Not alone the documentation of L'Affaire Georgina. It is insufficient. It is only one small part of the whole. There must be some way to express the kernel of twenty-seven years of petering-out. Though I am not far advanced in years, such tales could I tell . . . Why am I so tired? Who is Happiness? What is she? That all our swains commend her?

When she came out of the bathroom, wrapped in her towelling robe and feeling transparent, Haluk Bey was still sitting on the side of the bed, staring at the wall. He turned and looked at Maddy blankly.

'I feel very tired,' he said. His lips had stopped curling. His burgundy eyes looked the size of Buffalo nickels.

'Poor Haluk,' Maddy said, not knowing quite whether

she meant it. She might have meant it, it occurred to her. That would be strange and unaccountable, in the circumstances. Compassion forcing its way through a closed door.

He looked as if he might weep. He rubbed his prickly cheeks and chin. He patted the hair down over his ears. He occupied himself. The moment passed.

'Go and eat something,' Maddy said. 'You need food. You need a rest. Relax and quit hating us all. If you relax, you'll discover that you can't remember what any of us look like – past or present. That will refresh you. You'll be revived.'

'I must speak to Georgina,' he said. 'It is completely imperative.'

'I don't really think she wants to see you, Haluk. I simply don't think she understood about falling down the stairs.'

Haluk Bey groaned and lowered his head into his hands.

'Don't take it too hard,' Maddy said. 'Just think what it would have been like with Georgina after two or three years.' Maddy was caught up in this image for a full minute or two, during which time she was oblivious of Haluk Bey and the pea-green environs. 'You'll find someone nicer to play with,' she finally said.

He raised his head and looked at her. 'I am mad about Georgina,' he said. 'This morning, I am, yes. But by tonight . . . something comes over me.'

'Yes, well . . .' Maddy said.

'I am . . . changeable,' he said. He stared at the wall again for a few moments, his lips moving. 'My father was changeable also.'

'Well, I guess it's just genetic then, isn't it?' Maddy said. She walked over to the bureau and found a match for her cigarette. She pulled her tights and bra out of one drawer and skirt and sweater out of another and disappeared into the bathroom again. Shall I lock the door? She left it slightly ajar. She could hear Haluk Bey murmuring to himself. When she was dressed, she came out again. Haluk Bey looked away from his wall.

'Will you give her a message from me?' he said.

'Of course.'

'Tell her,' he said very calmly, 'that I wish her in hell for this betrayal. Tell her she will someday pay dearly for this cruelty. Will you remember to tell her?'

'Of course.'

'If she didn't get the message, I would be very disappointed.'

'I'm sure she'd hate to miss it too.'

He got up, straightening his misshapen jacket. 'Goodbye,' he said, bowing slightly. 'It has been a pleasure to meet you. I hope you have enjoyed your holiday here.'

Maddy opened the door for him. 'Oh, I have!' she said, as Haluk Bey moved slowly past her. 'It was everything a holiday could be. It was a true idyll. I feel like a nymph in one of those renaissance poems. Here I am, piping away in the glades.'

Haluk Bey's old malevolent smile struggled to force its way out through his little sharp teeth.

'You American women,' he said. 'You have a smart answer for everything . . .'

'Jesus . . .' Georgina said, her face stunned. 'Imagine. I'm just lucky I got off with a bruise.'

Gunzel was over at the weighing-in counter arguing with the clerk about her overweight bags. A delay in the flight time had already been announced.

'Jesus . . .' Georgina repeated. 'I just can't get over it.' She sat down weakly on the bench near where she and Maddy were standing. 'I just can't . . . I mean, what a nut! Leave it to me to get involved with the biggest nut in town. I've got a knack.'

'That's true,' Maddy said.

'God . . . imagine him coming up to your *room!*' The horror of it gripped Georgina's face. Her eyes snapped open like two shutters drawn. 'I would have been out of my mind,' she said. 'Weren't you scared?'

'No,' Maddy said. 'I wasn't anything at all, except a little sorry for him, at one point.'

'*Sorry* for him!' Georgina said.

'Are the lunatic not worthy of pity?' Maddy said.

'After what he did to me?' Georgina said, caressing her bruise.

'You provoke violence,' Maddy said calmly. 'I can understand the bruise without effort.'

'You really are a sadist, you know?' Georgina said. 'Like I've always said.'

Maddy smiled, feeling very distant and clear and unheated. Moving into the final stages – am I too smart for my own good? It's too soon to say . . . too soon. 'Names,' she said. 'All just names. Sticks and stones may break my bones . . .'

'Ah, God . . .' Gunzel said at her elbow. 'Forty extra liras to pay!'

Georgina pouted. Maddy smiled her distant smile. Gunzel looked from one to the other, then she slumped down next to Georgina on the bench and leaned her face in one gloved hand. 'I miss that Melek,' she said.

'Any word from her?' Georgina asked, staring woodenly across the terminal.

'A letter yesterday evening, special delivery,' Gunzel said. 'She has returned to her village. She says it is very cold in her room there. She says her fingers are so cold she almost cannot knit.'

Georgina looked up at Gunzel, the wooden face cracking,

life appearing in the fissures. 'You're kidding,' she said.

'Kidding?' Gunzel said. 'Why would I be kidding?'

'You mean,' Georgina said, 'that with a problem like hers – and buried alive in this village that's exactly nowhere – she writes to you about knitting!'

Maddy felt the laugh rising from somewhere deep down in her body. She couldn't identify the point of origin, it seemed to be gathering itself from every muscle and nerve. It emerged, irrepressible. She choked on its extremity. She coughed violently into the collar of her coat. She continued to laugh. Then it became a smile: soft and distant.

Gunzel and Georgina glared at her.

'Maddy is being unkind again,' Gunzel said to Georgina. 'She can be so nice when she is not being unkind.'

'Amen!' Georgina said.

Maddy blew hot steamy breaths into the tall collar of her coat, letting them deflect upon her face. It was very comforting. It was very private inside the collar, and comforting.

'There are a lot more nuts around here than meet the eye,' Georgina said, lighting a cigarette.

'I am glad to be leaving,' Gunzel said. 'It makes me nervous, this place.'

'I'm glad to be going back too,' Georgina said. She studied her fingernails. 'What are you doing for Christmas?' she said to Gunzel. 'Going anywhere?' She smiled her brightest smile, her eyebrows rising the millimeter left them.

'Chapter One,' Maddy whispered inside her coat collar: a soft, steamy whisper. 'Is Chapter One too soon to consider the question of Vulnerability? The Value of Vulnerability – maybe I'll call it that. It has a nice alliterative ring: the Value of Vulnerability. Has it any value? It exposes the nerves – is that valuable? Should the nerves be safely tucked away? Is anyone safe? *Should* anyone be safe? Perhaps it's all too . . . maybe Chapter One is too soon . . . how could it be too soon?'

Gunzel's little smile trembled in and out of existence like dust in a sunbeam. 'What is she saying?' she said to Georgina.

Georgina looked bored. 'Who cares?' she said. 'Listen, Gunzel . . . about Christmas . . .'

'Chapter Two,' Maddy whispered to her collar, 'will be called – Emptiness Plus Opportunity: the Modern Personality. Is that too condensed? Perhaps I could . . . A subsidiary question – how can emptiness be permeated? Empty things can be filled but how can empty people be filled? What you stick in just drifts out again, nothing sticky to hold it. Filled is not a good word. It's all getting . . .'

'We could take a night flight,' Georgina said. 'They're cheaper.'

'Ah, the sun . . . the sea . . .' Gunzel exclaimed, smiling dreamily.

'It is all going too fast,' Maddy confided to the silky lining that lay almost against her lips. 'At this rate my memoirs will be over in three or four chapters. Too concentrated. I must expand. Expatiate. No need to be so succinct. How can you be succinct when you are dealing with petering-out? Petering-out is interminable.'

'It overlooks the Med,' Georgina said. 'Lovely view from all the rooms. A friend of mine stayed there last –'

'What is she saying?' Gunzel interrupted, pointing at Maddy standing at the end of the bench with her neck drawn down into her coat collar, her hands stuffed deep into her pockets. 'Is she speaking to us? Has she gone mad, do you think?'

'Pay no attention,' Georgina said. 'It's just a goddamn act.'

'Act?' Gunzel said uncertainly. 'It's an act?'

'Perhaps,' Maddy whispered into the collar, 'I could say a word or two about prevalent sexual and emotional habits, in a general way. I could call that part – the Merry-Go-Round. That's a trifle mundane. Maybe the Glass-Eyed Teddy Bear would be better. Is it better?'

Gunzel tapped her feet and studied the floor. She snapped her handbag open and shut. Georgina had fallen silent, smoking without interruption.

'Stop doing that,' Georgina said, without turning her head.

'Doing what?' Gunzel said.

'What you're doing with your feet,' Georgina said. 'And your hands. Can't you sit still? Jesus . . . you're a nervous wreck.'

'I think Maddy is not well,' Gunzel said solemnly. 'If she was well she would not stand there mumbling to herself like that. It's not normal to do such things.'

Georgina turned, bored, and looked towards Maddy. 'It's all an act, take my word for it,' she said loudly. 'Just an act. Forget it. Just ignore her. Think about something else.'

'What else?' Gunzel said, twitching. 'I'm sorry but you know this waiting drives me just crazy.'

'So you said before,' Georgina said.

Gunzel looked chastened. 'I'm sorry,' she repeated.

'It's all right,' Georgina said.

'However, I don't wish to speak in a general, disembodied way,' Maddy said, feeling her warm breath bounce back on the base of her nose. 'I wish to speak only in a very personal voice. After all, these are memoirs. I shall omit the Glass-Eyed Teddy Bear. Yes. Instead, I will call it – Grandmother's Eye Blinks Gold for Yes and Red for No. Subtitled: Madam X, or the Izmir Idyll.'

'Give me a cigarette,' Gunzel said.

'Oh God . . .' Georgina said.

'I'm nervous. I must have a cigarette to make me calm.'

'Here,' Georgina said. 'Now, for God's sake blow the other way.'

Gunzel smoked, watching Maddy out of the corner of her eye. 'It's not an act,' she said after a few minutes. 'She is not well. Why doesn't she sit down?'

'Because she prefers to stand,' Georgina said. 'You get more attention standing than sitting.'

Gunzel puffed violently. 'Georgina . . .'

'Listen,' Georgina said, 'if you want to do something about her, go ahead and do it. But count me out. I'm not taking anymore of her insults.'

Gunzel got up, holding the back of the bench to steady herself. She walked over and stood at Maddy's elbow for a moment, looking at the floor and listening. She pulled at Maddy's sleeve. Maddy lifted her head out of its cocoon.

'On the other hand, I could subsume everybody under the single heading – the Distant Eye as a Component of Essential Absence. I think that's rather fine.' She turned to Gunzel. She smiled. 'All the chapters interconnect beautifully so far. It's a masterwork.'

'Why are you standing here with your mouth in your collar saying these things to yourself?' Gunzel said. 'Are you not well?'

'I am going to be sick in a new way,' Maddy said. 'One must keep moving. That's all I can tell you.'

'Maddy . . .'

'I am pulling up the drawbridge around the castle. I shall live in my head with a distant view of the town.'

Gunzel walked the length of the bench again and sat down next to Georgina, who was still smoking furiously but with an outward appearance of calm.

'I cannot understand what she's saying,' Gunzel said. 'It all sounds very funny.'

'I bet it does,' Georgina said. 'She's probably composing another little bit of character assassination. She's good at that.'

Gunzel fidgeted, shuffling her feet back and forth under the bench. She massaged the glossy sides of her handbag. She opened the handbag and took out an envelope and stared at it and then put it back in the bag again. 'This waiting drives me –'

'I know, I know,' Georgina said. 'Go and see if the flight's about ready to be called.'

Gunzel got up, ran her hands down the sides of her skirt, and teetered over to the ticket counter.

Georgina turned her head and looked at Maddy. 'You can cut that out now,' she said. 'Your audience has left. Relax.' She heard a small breathless laugh emanate from inside the high collar at the end of the bench. She got up, put the hand that wasn't holding her cigarette into the big patch pocket of her coat, and walked unhurriedly down to Maddy. She stood very near her, watching with a slight icy smile, her eyebrows pulling her eyes up into little oblique slits. She ran her hand slowly over one side of her hair and over the thick roll of hair at the nape of her neck without taking her eyes off Maddy. 'Listen, Maddy . . .' she said, 'don't you think you've gone far enough with this little performance? I mean, *I* know you're perfectly all right but some people might think you've gone running mad. How would you like to be shut up in a Turkish asylum? Remember those lovely pictures?'

Maddy withdrew her head from its comfort, its privacy, and looked at Georgina. 'It's very difficult,' she said. 'I'm only to Chapter Five, after all this concentration.'

Georgina lowered her cigarette. 'Chapter Five?'

'From a projected fifteen chapters,' Maddy said. 'I like

the number fifteen. For some reason.'

'What the hell are you talking about?'

'No need to say,' Maddy said. 'No need even to try to say. Privacy, that's the thing. The private head. The head living on its own. Is that possible? Can I preserve myself with the very Instruments of Death?'

Georgina dropped her cigarette on the floor. She moved back two steps. 'Snap out of it, Maddy,' she said. 'You can't do this.'

Maddy smiled. 'Are we ready to go?'

Georgina turned and looked for Gunzel. 'Wait a minute. I'll go see.' Maddy watched her go to the ticket counter and speak to Gunzel. They both turned and looked at her, silent and thoughtful. Maddy smiled at them across the room. Why not? What did it matter?

Georgina returned. 'Ten minutes, we can board,' she said.

'Lovely,' Maddy said.

'You all right now?'

'Never better,' Maddy said. 'Never, ever better.'

'Want a cigarette?'

Maddy shook her head. She sat down on the end of the bench, watching the passengers preparing to board the plane. Stretching themselves, gathering up bags. Calling children. Stepping on cigarettes.

'Chapter Fifteen,' she said, 'the last chapter, will be entitled – Flight. Just – Flight. No subtitles.'

Georgina shook her head. 'Jesus . . .' she said.

Gunzel came over, clutching her handbag, watching Maddy apprehensively. 'Is she all right?' she said to Georgina in a low voice.

Maddy smiled. 'Dear girl,' she said.

Gunzel hesitated for a moment and then touched Maddy's arm. 'My dear friend Maddy,' she said.

'Now, isn't that touching . . .' Georgina said.

'Meaningless,' Maddy said, still smiling. 'Just meaningless. A gesture at the precipice. But I'm not fooled.'

'You need to see a doctor,' Georgina said.

'Perhaps . . .' Gunzel began, 'if you –'

'Shall we board our plane?' Maddy said. 'Shall we join the others in flight?'

The three of them proceeded to the gates, presented their boarding passes, and walked out into the bright day with its November chill in the air.

'Just a minute, just a minute!' Gunzel yelled. She turned and rushed over to the outside barrier. She snatched up the bouquet Hasan Bey held forward and hurried back again, turning once to wave. She looked straight ahead, avoiding Maddy's eyes, holding the bouquet with both hands, like a good-luck charm.

'Chapter Five . . .' Maddy breathed into her collar, feeling the warm breath enclose her face, knowing she smiled because of the cold air against her teeth. 'Chapter Five – Love. Subtitles undetermined.'